THE TAKACSES OF HUNGARY

Proving God's Faithfulness

Thank you David, for your prayers and pastoral help. It is God blessings to know you.

Rose

Rose Takacs Little

with Helen Jordan Davis

The Takacses of Hungary: Proving God's Faithfulness

by Rose Takacs Little with Helen Jordan Davis

ISBN: 978-0-9961897-2-9
Ebook ISBN: 978-0-9961897-3-6

Published by: Principle Books Publishers

Cover design by: Tina Schinneller of Image Media Resource. Painting on front cover by Paul Takacs.

First Printing: June, 2018

Printed in the United States of America

Dedication

This book is dedicated to Almighty God for His mercy and grace that protected and blessed this family through so much.

Rose Takacs Little with Helen Jordan Davis

Foreword

"A powerfully moving story of the sovereignty and faithfulness of God in the lives of a family trapped in the horrors of war. A reminder to us all that God is always with us, always at work in our lives, always loving us. The strength of the Takacs family has endured throughout generations. A testimony to persevering and trusting God in the worst of times and the best of times. A must read that I highly recommend."

—*Rev. Linda Parker*

"A story well worth telling!" —*Ward Harris*

"Ward and I visited Hungary, and in particular Budapest, in 2005. Huba, Rose's brother-in-law, was our private guide and was very impressive with his knowledge of the history of his country. He took us to so many famous places in two days that our brains were swirling! One night he had his son, Balazs, who was driving a cab at the time, pick us up and take us to a restaurant high up on a hill on the Pest side of the city. We met Huba and Zsuzsi there and enjoyed a lovely dinner accompanied by a Hungarian trio of violins and guitar. Special!"

—*Auleen Harris*

"I have been blessed to know the Takacs family for many years. This is a story that needed to be told. Thank you, Rose, for keeping it alive." —*Rev. David Sheffield*

"A true story of a family's endurance in overcoming hardships that gives a glimpse into a world that most Westerners know little about."

—*Kammy Davis*

Prologue

Hungary Escape Filled With Terror

By Zsolt B. Takacs

The black, soot-covered engine was shaking toward the border towns of Hungary—pulling a full load of people filled with hope and expectations toward a new beginning in the West.

I was sitting on one of the smoke-filled cars surrounded by darkly dressed people of all ages. A low murmur of voices could be heard around me. Most of these dark figures were clutching to them a few precious reminders of their home—perhaps all of their earthly possessions.

It was a frightful sight for a 17-year-old boy who had to grow up fast in these terrifying days of October, 1956.

Suddenly the realization of being alone but surrounded by strangers dawned on me. "What am I doing here?" I wondered. "What will the future hold in store for me?" The logical answer quickly drowned out the doubtful, silent cries from within. This was the question of survival—I had to escape.

Earlier that morning I left our house to "look around" my beloved city, which was a routine task in those days. School was not in session since the authorities were still confused and most government machines were at a standstill after the revolution.

The gallant effort of a whole nation was lost and there was nothing to do but wait until the unwanted regime got back in power and started its revengeful collections on all the people.

The dialogue also was routine between my mother and me. "Where are you going?" she asked. "When are you coming back?" The answer blurted out of me automatically. "I am going out, but will be home for lunch," I said to pacify and reassure her. Actually, we were all looking forward to lunch, which almost always consisted of hot soup, because it felt good after hours in the bitter cold.

After walking around the city several hours, meeting with friends, collecting news and rumors, I was heading back on foot, walking hurriedly under stately chestnut trees, but carefully enough not to step on loose cobble stones which could mean a slip or annoying injury.

Taking a shortcut through the churchyard, I could already see our house standing on a slope—about 300 yards away. Suddenly my heart stopped! There were soldiers, police and civilians around our house and especially at our front door. The reason for their being there came to me without having to think about it. They had already started rounding up all those who had voiced their opposition to their merciless system.

I followed my first instinct. I turned and ran to the railroad station and kept hoping that a train would leave which could help me get to the western border where I would try to get out and into Austria—a free country.

I felt lucky that day to see the commotion around my house before the police noticed me. Good fortune was still with me when I arrived at the depot and saw people piling on a train which had already started to make its way out of the covered structure. I could not and did not hesitate in jumping on the platform, holding onto the cold railing with all my nervous strength.

To my surprise, no one ever came and collected for tickets. I never saw the conductor until we reached the so-called "Border Zone." (Editor's note: the "Border Zone" stretched along the border between Hungary and Austria, and consisted of mine fields, barbed wire and guard houses all ostensibly designed to keep people from infiltrating into Hungary.)

The train started to slow down amid corn fields before the scheduled last stop, where we all knew that only people with special permits were allowed. The conductor now appeared, yelling to all those without papers to jump. The corn fields were already peppered with black, moving figures, running, stopping and running again.

By the time the slow-crawling train pushed forward a short distance, most of the people, including me, were trying to corner the best cover the fields had to offer. I had jumped right after a man who had two infants in his arms. Desperation showed all around me, but we all landed safely.

There were no voices heard anywhere now. Only the crunching sound of frozen snow under my feet and sounds of carelessly broken corn stalks trampled by scared, running human beings. It was dark and very cold.

In the distance, dogs were barking. Once in a while, flashlights broke the darkness, followed by shouting and some distant gunfire, then silence again. Looking at my watch in the dark, I realized it was 10 o'clock and that I had walked for four hours. Some trees appeared nearby, giving me new hope for good camouflage.

My stomach struck some discordant chords since I had had nothing but snow to eat since 8 that morning. Reaching the woods, I found myself very tired and wanting to go to sleep.

The dog barks had not subsided and this gave me extra incentive to tear into the forest as far as I could.

Suddenly, fear surrounded me. Could I be unfortunate enough to step on a field mine? Could they track me with dogs? Would I freeze and die before I was found? Secretly, I started to hope that the border guards would capture me.

My 17-year-old logic and the prevailing "know-it-all" attitude took over, telling me that it could not happen to me and that I would be in Austria shortly and it would be all right. I had to forge forward.

Out of the dark, a harsh voice boomed out from behind me. "Stop, don't move, put your hands up or you will be shot!" Oh, God, I thought, he let me pass him to see if I was armed and alone and only then he dared to stop me. "Coward!" I said under my breath as I was standing there. I was proven wrong, however, when in seconds I was surrounded by uniformed men pointing their guns at me.

One of them started to talk to me, asking me what I was doing coming from Austria and where did I think I was going. I told them I was trying to get to Austria and not coming from there. This answer must have amused them because a muffled laughter came from the group's direction, followed by an explanation that I was probably lost in the dark, circling into Austria and back (crossing the mine field twice).

At the border station, two soldiers shoved me into a room full of people—the same stuffy air and smoke greeted me as on the train. They caught the whole bunch, I thought to myself, starting to find some humor in this "here we go again" situation.

The next 2 ½ days were the most horrifying days of my life. We were given absolutely no food. We had to use a corner of our room as a toilet and a bucket of water a day for 25 people. Civilized people would never understand this.

Finally my turn came as they led me into a separate office and questioned me at length. Standing up was a real effort now and slowly falling little dots were marching in front of my eyes. After this newest ordeal was over, I was treated to some bread and milk which almost made me sick, after gulping down every bite.

The lieutenant in charge told me that I should be ashamed of myself for worrying my parents. Then he slapped me across the face and ordered me into a troop carrier to be taken back to Budapest.

My resistance was gone by now and all I could think about was some hot soup to make my starving body respond to my thoughts.

The driver and the armed guard seemed to be totally disinterested in us. Several people begged them to let us out, let us go, let us go free, but to no avail.

We hardly left the station when all of a sudden the truck stopped and we were encircled by armed men and women, obviously some broken off segment of a group of Freedom Fighters, who ordered the soldiers to get out, then helped guide us to the other side of the border.

It never occurred to me then that I would ever get out alive. Darkness had surrounded us once again as the forced march began. An eternity later, we were told that the lights blinking sleepily in the distance were the lights of Austria. It did not seem to matter anymore.

Once again, a voice from the dark (not as harsh, however) informed us—this time in halting Hungarian—that for the past 15 minutes we had been on the Austrian side.

All 30 of us, without any words or any special cue, fell on our knees and said our special thanks and prayers. It was November 27 at 12:01 a.m.

The events that followed were going much faster than those four days spent in horror. Communications with Hungary were nonexistent and on March 7, 1957 I was graciously accepted by the United States as a refugee.

The very first trip I made back to Vienna was five years later, to meet my sister and her husband at a special 48-hour tour to see a soccer game. Borrowing money, I took this opportunity to see someone from my family, my own flesh and blood.

All the way from New York to Vienna, I was trying to find a way to greet them—wondering what my sister might say. Will she scold me? Will she be happy to see me? Will she bring good news of my parents?

Waiting nervously at the train station, all of my uncertainties were answered and dispersed when the joyful, tearful reunion started with a silent hug and kiss. Through the tears, my sister's first words were: "Mother is sending you this message. She wants you to know that she loves you and that your soup has gotten cold."

(Zsolt Takacs's story was published in The Florida Times-Union Jacksonville Journal newspaper in the Sunday, October 28, 1979 edition. The following information was added at that time by the paper's reporter.)

In late October of 1956, the Hungarian government was thrown into turmoil by a citizens' revolt which, for a short period, succeeding in overthrowing the ruling communists.

Zsolt B. Takacs was then a 17-year-old college student and member of one of the student groups protesting in sympathetic demonstrations against the jailing of Polish students. These groups were later tagged by the press as Hungary's Freedom Fighters.

As the revolt began to fail and government troops returned to embattled Budapest in November to arrest those involved in the revolt, Takacs fled the country as did two of his brothers, none of whom knew the others had escaped until later.

Takacs's father, a member of the opposition to the communists, was arrested and sentenced to death before intervention by American and Japanese authorities managed to get his sentence commuted to life imprisonment. He was released 6½ years later after he developed leukemia, heart trouble and cancer.

Of six children in the Takacs family, four are now living in the free world—the three brothers who escaped in 1956 and a sister, who defected to the United States in late 1974. Takacs's mother and a younger brother and sister are still living in Hungary.

Takacs, who became a citizen of the United States in December 1961, is now a Jacksonville resident and manager of the "At Need Department" at Restlawn Cemetery.

This is the story of his escape.[1]

This book will follow the Takacs family, a Christian family, and see how it fared under the various governments controlling the nation of Hungary. More about Zsolt's story and the Revolution of 1956 in Chapter 7.

The story in this book is told by Rose Takacs Little, with contributions from Zsolt Takacs, in 2017-2018, and will show the faithfulness of God to preserve His people in times of deep trouble.

"At the right time, God always dropped the right people

into our lives to help us." —Rose Takacs Little

"Historically, Hungary's resiliency in the face of adversity has been non

parallel. The history of my country of origin is like a Liszt Rhapsody:

beautiful, moving, full of joy and suffering, and always ending on a

soaring note. Rising like the Phoenix from the ashes." [2] —Zsolt Takacs

Table of Contents

Introduction

After almost 200 years of being controlled by Ottoman Muslim, Nazi, or Communist rule, free and independent Hungary has returned to its roots of being a bastion of Christianity.

Part of Hungary's problem was that it was such a beautiful and productive land that it attracted foreign powers who wanted to possess it. On the banks of the beautiful Danube River, Buda on one bank and Pest on the other, combined in 1848 as Budapest, the city was considered by many to be the most beautiful in all of Europe. In the 15th century, it became a center of Renaissance culture. The control of this beautiful land has changed hands many times over the past 2,000 years, now returning officially to its Christian roots established 1,000 years ago.

As we follow the story of one family, we will also examine a brief history of Hungary, condensed from encyclopedia and Internet articles and displayed throughout the book in italics to separate it from the main text.

In the 6th century BC Scythians from the Black Sea region settled here, and there are signs of Celto-Illyrian tribes having been here in the 4th/3rd century BC.[3]

The region of Hungary was once a Roman province, which was overrun by Germanic tribes in the 2nd century AD. These Germanic tribes were in turn driven out by the Huns. After Attila the Hun died, the Germanic tribes returned until the 5th century, when they were expelled by an Asian people, the Avars. During the 8th century, the Moravians, a Slavic people, took over the north and east, while Charlemagne, king of the Franks, took the remainder of the territory in 797. In 895-896, a Finno-Ugric tribe known as the Magyars seized control.[4]

The Takacs family, whose story is told in this book, are Magyars, as is the preponderance of the populace still today.

> *After some battles with the Holy Roman Empire, friendlier relations were established between the two, and Christianity and Western culture penetrated Hungary. Duke Geza converted to Christianity in 975, and his son, Stephen I, received recognition as King of Hungary in 1001, being given the title of Apostolic Majesty by Pope Sylvester II. Stephen was canonized in 1083, and Christianity became the official religion of the country.*[5]

Today, Hungary has returned to these Christian roots, some calling this a new Renaissance. The following information on the Hungarian government's protection of Christianity today is taken from the CBN News program, "Jerusalem Dateline," shown on GOD TV, August 28, 2017.[6]

Since Hungary is a member of the European Union, the EU is trying to force Hungary to accept swarms of undocumented Muslim immigrants, even after seeing the terror and chaos this has produced in other European nations. With its establishment as a Christian nation around the year 1000, Hungary freely allowed other faiths to function unhampered, never dictating what faith should be followed. Over the years, however, Islam, Nazism, or Communism have at times gained control, with Christianity not being given the same protection it had given others, but being squelched by each of these, along with their persecution of Jews. Hungary is determined to never again allow Christianity to be so treated.

Today, Hungary has re-written its Constitution to protect and nourish the family and to protect Christian values, such as marriage being between a man and a woman and life beginning at conception, and states explicitly, "God bless the Hungarians." The Pentecostal Church in Hungary is thriving. The government has set up an office to help persecuted Christians worldwide, saying that taking in persecuted Christians is its moral and constitutional duty.

Except when the Nazis, the Muslims, or the Communists were in control, Jews have always found a safe haven in Hungary, free from persecution, though, as always, there has been a measure of prejudice on the part of some.

Today, the government is unabashedly Christian, with its Prime Minister, Viktor Orban being an outspoken Christian. For being a Christian, for saying that the European Union is trying to "Islamize" Europe, the head of the EU calls Orban a "dictator."

Hungary is a landlocked country, surrounded by Austria, Slovakia, Ukraine, Romania, Serbia, Croatia, and Slovenia. It is tiny compared to the huge European Union to which it belongs and to which it is offering resistance by supporting Christianity. David facing Goliath again.

Chapter One: Ancestors

We've seen the founding of the nation of Hungary and its Christian roots, with Stephen I being made King of Hungary in 1001. It later grew to be a very powerful nation.

A later leader, Ladislas, subjugated Croatia, Bosnia, and part of Transylvania, and his successor obtained part of Dalmatia. Hungary was then a powerful kingdom, which developed a feudal system and nobility, with landowners holding huge areas of land.

Serbia and more of Bosnia were added in the 1300s. When a Hungarian king married the sister of the king of Poland, Poland was brought into the kingdom, and Hungary became one of the largest realms of Europe. Reforms were made promoting commerce, science, and industry, and some of the powers of the feudal lords were curbed.

The Ottoman Turks (Muslims) seized some of the fringe territory in the late 1300s, finally being driven out in 1456.

Matthais Corvinus became king in 1458 and took control of Austria from the Habsburgs, moving his residence to Vienna. He later acquired Moravia, Silesia, and Lusatia, making Hungary the strongest kingdom in central Europe.

Under Corvinus, Buda became a center of Renaissance culture.[7]

Now the Muslims returned. The Turkish army under Sultan Suleiman I crushed the Hungarian army and captured Buda in 1526. Austria's Habsburg Holy Roman Emperors regained control of the western part of the kingdom, while the Turks controlled the central part, and the Magyars remained in control of Transylvania.

With the Reformation came strife between the Protestant Magyars and the Catholic Habsburgs, with the Magyars gaining religious autonomy and additional territory by 1606. By 1644, full religious freedom was granted to all Hungarians under Habsburg rule. By 1682, the Habsburg Austrians had virtually driven the Turks from Hungary, as the Turks retained only a small region, which they lost 19 years later. The crown of Hungary was declared forever hereditary in the house of the Austrian Habsburgs.

In 1703, Hungarians rebelled against Austrian rule, and in 1711, peace terms provided for a general amnesty, religious freedom, and numerous political concessions, with the Austrian Habsburgs still in control. Things remained calm for a century, then in 1815, a resurgence of Hungarian nationalism began. The Liberal Party was formed, demanding a constitutional government and other reforms. Commoners became eligible for public office, and certain feudal restrictions on the peasantry were curtailed. In 1847, political groups in Hungary threatened a revolution, so the Habsburgs agreed to a Hungarian Ministry with a Hungarian Premier. This ministry soon severed almost all ties with Austria, and Hungarian became the national language. In April of 1849, Hungary declared independence.

Austria quickly made an alliance with Russia, and by August, the rebellion of Hungary was squelched. Austria ruled there again.

Austria was weakened in 1859 by a defeat in the Italian War of Liberation and in 1865 agreed to a new constitution for Hungary. Before the new constitution could be completed, Prussia defeated Austria, and in 1867, Austria and Hungary became a dual monarchy, the Austro-Hungarian Empire.[8]

Eordoghs

Now we come to the period during which Rose Takacs Little's maternal grandparents, Zoltan Eordogh (1885-1953) and Margit Puly Eordogh (1881-1919), lived. The Eordogh family has been traced back to the 1200s.[9]

Eordogh Coat of Arms, 1250[10]

Zoltan Eordogh (left) playing polo 1907

Margit and Zoltan Eorgogh[11]

Margit's parents were Janos Puly (1841- ?) and Sarolta Vlasits Puly (1854 - ?).[12]

Janos Puly[13]

Sarolta Puly[14]

Janos was a banker and an aristocrat, the equivalent of a Baron. His motorcar, a Ford, shown here in 1904, is said to be the first in all of Hungary.

Janos Puly[15]

Margit and Zoltan Eordogh's daughter, Rozsa Eordogh, was born in 1909 and married Dr. Pal Takacs in 1929. Their family is the one whose lives are followed in our story.

Takacs-Micskey

Dr. Takacs of our story, the father of Ferenc, Paul, Rose, Zsolt, Attila, and Zsuzsanna, is the son of Ferenc Takacs (1841-1914) and Terezia Micskey Takacs (1859-1932).[16]

Ferenc Takacs[17]

Terezia Micskey Takacs[18]

Ferenc Takacs was a lawyer whose son, Aurel, also a lawyer, helped Dr. Takacs through medical school.

Aurel Takacs[19]

Takacs Coat of Arms

Terezia's parents were Daniel Micskey (1821-?) and Julianna Pogany Micskey (1832-?).[20]

The Micskey family was aristocratic, having a Coat of Arms dating to the 1600s.

Micskey Coat of Arms[21]

Ferenc (Frank) Takacs, Rose's oldest brother, gave the original document of the Coat of Arms of the Micskey family, pictured above, to Zsolt's oldest son, Thomas, as a wedding present. He had it examined at a museum in New York where he was told it has great value, having been signed by King Leopold. The wax seal into which King Leopold's signet was impressed is still intact. Thomas was instructed to always keep the document under glass to protect it.

Chapter Two: Rozsa Eordogh

In WWI, the Hungarian political leaders supported the Austrian war effort because they were afraid a Russian victory would mean a dismemberment of their country. Food shortages and other privations caused unrest among the populace until on Oct. 25, 1917 a national council was established, parliament was dissolved, and Hungary made peace with the Allies. In Nov. of 1918, the national council proclaimed the Hungarian Democratic Republic. This government was overthrown by the Communists in 1919, and the government confiscated all industrial and commercial enterprises as communal property. Banks were taken over, and many newspapers were banned.[22]

Rozsa Eordogh, Rose Little's mother, was born in 1909, the oldest child of Zoltan and Margit Eordogh.

Rozsa Eordogh

Nine-year-old Rozsa, her father, her pregnant mother, and her two younger brothers, Zoltan, seven years old, and Tibor, five years old, were living in Transylvania when Romania captured the area and established communism there. The year was 1918. The Romanians were killing Hungarians, so the Eordoghs packed up what they could and fled, planning to locate near Margit's parents, who lived on a lake outside of Budapest.

Though they managed to escape the Romanian Communists, they still faced tragedy. As soon as they had settled in the small town of Szekszard, the family awoke one morning to find that pregnant Margit had died during the night, having had a heart attack while asleep.

Young Zoltan, Zoltan, Tibor, Rozsa Eordogh [23]

To compound the tragedy, Rozsa's father was arrested and put in jail on charges trumped up by the Communists, who had gained control of this area as well. Margit's father, Janos Puly, an aristocrat, was the Director of a bank. The Communists were suspicious of people with such standing, and Zoltan, being new in the area and connected to this family, was a natural target for them.

The authorities who took him in were so heartless they failed to find someone to care of the children, leaving nine-year-old Rozsa to care for herself and her two younger brothers. Her grandparents at the lake, who were on their way there, though they didn't know about the arrest, were delayed by the Communists, further compounding the problem.

Rozsa cared for the two boys and herself, not knowing how long her father would be gone. Fortunately, her father only remained in jail for about a week. He later got a job working for the Government Agricultural Ministry as an overseer, while also developing a vineyard on his own land.

Upheaval

Now the Czechs invaded Hungary from the north, and the Romanians invaded from the south. The Communist leader fled to Austria, and Romanians took over Budapest. Soon the Allies took supervision and established an interim government with participation from all political parties. The Allies insisted on general elections in early 1920. The national assembly severed all ties with Austria, proclaiming the country a monarchy. Hungary accepted the Treaty of Trianon, imposed by the Allies, which deprived Hungary of Transylvania, Croatia, and Slovakia.[24]

By comparing the map of Hungary before the treaty took away land with the map afterwards, one can see why these terms seemed humiliating to the Hungarians. Hungary lost 72% of its land and lost its seaport. Rose and Zsolt see it as though parts of the country had been amputated, leaving the country crippled, severely diminished. The boundaries set then are the boundaries of the country today.

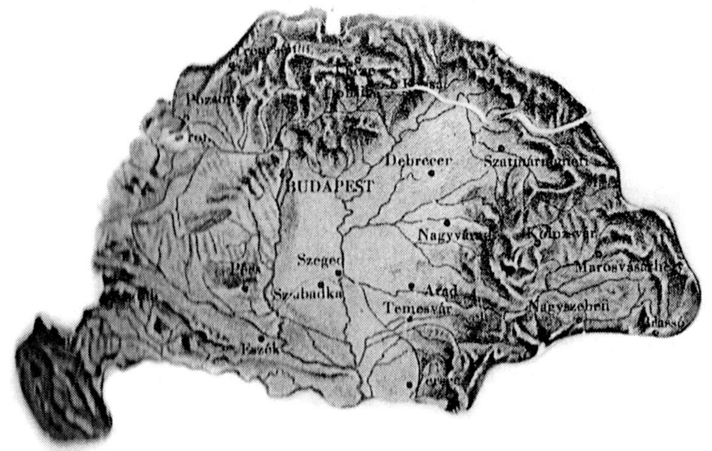

Map Before Treaty [25]

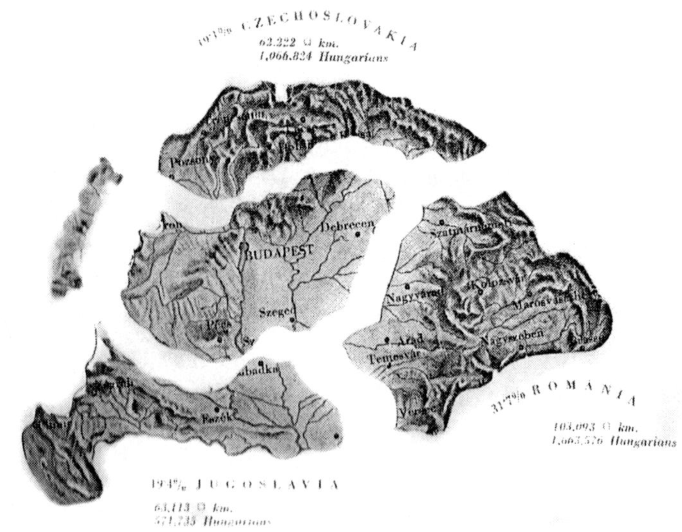

Map After Treaty [26]

The small part in the middle indicates Hungary after the Treaty and shows the boundaries of Hungary today.

Life Goes On

In 1922, Rozsa's father re-married. The step-mother, Matilde, loved Rozsa and her brothers dearly and was very good to them. She also bore Rozsa's father three more children: Bertalan, Arpad, and Katalin.

Matilde and Zoltan Eordogh[27]

Bertalan Eordogh[28]

Arpad Eordogh[29]

Katalin Eordogh[30]

When Rozsa was 19 years old, her best friend's family moved from the small town, Szekszard, to Budapest. There was a new young doctor there, a very eligible bachelor, who the friend's family thought would make a perfect mate for their daughter. They began to plan occasions for the two young people to be thrown together, becoming very aggressive with their machinations. Nothing seemed to be working, though. Now Rozsa came to visit her friend. One look at her and the young doctor said, "I'm going to marry you." At first Rozsa was stubborn and refused his attentions, but after two years of persistence on his part, they were married on June 1, 1929. The young doctor was Pal Janos Laszlo Takacs.

Wedding of Rozsa Eordogh and Dr. Pal Takacs

Chapter Three:
Dr. Pal Takacs

Dr. Pal (pronounced like Paul) Janos Laszlo Takacs had known some difficulty in his life, as well. He was born in Debrecen, Hungary, a town near the Romanian border, on March 21, 1900 to Ferenc and Terezia Takacs. When Pal was 14 years old, his father, a lawyer, died. Fortunately he had an older brother who was also a lawyer, who could help him and his mother. The older brother, Aurel, made sure Pal finished High School, and he then helped him through the Semmelweis Institute of the Scientists University of Budapest to fulfill the dream of becoming a doctor.

The university studies took six years, then Pal had one year as an Intern. On completion of his studies, the young doctor took a job at a private citizens' clinic in Budapest, caring for government officials, actors, and other "important" people. At the same time, he also worked in the Hungarian Railroad company clinic and joined the military reserves.

Life In Spite of Politics

So Dr. Pal Takacs and Rozsa Eordogh married in 1929.

Dr. Takacs's mother, Terezia, had a disabled sister, Irma, who lived with her. Before Terezia died, she told Pal he must always take care of Irma, who was deaf and had a hunchback. Pal of course agreed, and Irma lived with Dr. Takacs's family until she died at age 84.

By 1932, there was a resurgence of Hungarian nationalism which fostered aggressive foreign policy toward neighboring democracies and led to closer relations with the totalitarian regimes of Fascist Italy and Nazi Germany.[31]

Government officials were moving Hungary in the wrong direction. This would prove devastating in the future.

Rozsa had been excommunicated from the Catholic Church when she married Dr. Takacs, because he was not Catholic. The Takacs family attended the Reformed Presbyterian Church, which Dr. Takacs had helped his good friend, Istvan Demjen, establish. Even though Rozsa had been excommunicated, they also attended the Catholic Church services. The Catholic Church was very ornate and impressive, in contrast to the Reformed church, which was very plain.

Shortly after the first son, Ferenc, was born, Dr. Takacs bought a large, expensive bell for the Reformed Church belfry to express his gratitude to God. He was in his early 30s at the time, fairly new in his practice, so this expensive gift was not given out of excessive luxury. Sadly, years later the Nazis confiscated it to make a canon from its metal. The son in whose name the gift had been given replaced it in 2002.

The first photo shows young Ferenc with the original bell as it was given in 1933, the second shows Istvan Demjen, the church pastor, along with Rozsa Takacs, nine-year-old Rose, Attila (crying) and Zsuzanna saying goodbye to the bell as it was about to be taken away by the Germans. The third shows the replacement bell, which remains in the church today.

Ferenc with the Bell, 1933 [32]   Bell Being Taken Away [33]

New Bell, Replaced by Ferenc in 2002

Demjen pastored the Reformed Presbyterian Church, and when Rose was born, he became her Godfather. When she was a few years older, Demjen's wife, Rose's Godmother, taught her the Catechism. Her brothers had similar classes, and there were programs in the summer similar to Vacation Bible Schools that are held in the US. For two years Ferenc and Paul attended a famous boarding school in Sarospatak. The school was run by the Reformed Presbyterian Church, with Reformed pastors as teachers, and had the prestige that Princeton has in America. If you graduated from there, you were considered to have it made for the future. When the country was being so severely bombed in 1944, Dr. Takacs felt it would be better to keep the family together, so he brought the boys home.

Ferenc Takacs 1944

Paul Takacs 1944

Chapter Four:
Family Life

Rose Ildiko (named Rozsa after her mother, but Americanized to Rose after her defection to America) Takacs was born in Budapest, Hungary on May 28, 1935 to Pal Takacs, MD, General Practitioner, and his wife, Rozsa Eordogh Takacs, following two older brothers: Ferenc Pal, born in 1930, and Pal Gyotgy (later Americanized to Paul), born in 1932. She was followed by two other brothers, Zsolt Bence, born in 1939, and Attila Tibor, born in 1942. A sister, Zsuzsanna Maria, was born in 1945.

Takacs Family Before Zsuzsy Was Born
Rose, Attila, Mother Rozsa, Ferenc, Zsolt, Dr. Takacs, Paul

Rose, Paul, Ferenc 1939[34]

Atilla, Rose, Zsolt 1943[35]

The Takacs were a close, happy, upper-middle-class family until World War II reached Hungary. Dr. and Mrs. Takacs frequently attended concerts, operas, and other cultural events, as did others in their social class. The children had the run of their small town, called Budafok, where they lived on the outskirts of Budapest. Everyone knew everyone else, and people all over town knew these were the children of their beloved doctor, called "Uncle Pal" by everyone.

When Dr. Takacs would call "Rozsa," both Rose and her mother would answer. If he wanted young Rose, he would say, "Not you, the little one." The word for "little one" is "Kicsi," so to the family, Rose became Kicsi, the family name for her still today.

The children grew up on the classical music of Liszt and Bartok. When Dr. Takacs and Rozsa would return home from a concert, Dr. Takacs would often sit down at the piano and play the songs they had just heard. He did this from memory without the written music. For three years Rose took piano lessons, but no one in the family seemed to have the gift for music the doctor had. Rose still loves classical music and has it playing daily in her home.

They lived in a comfortable house with a huge backyard, large enough for a big garden, pens for hogs, swings, plenty of play space for the children, and a creek at the back of the lot. The doctor always encouraged the children to invite their friends over, so there was always a wonderful crowd around. They had everything they needed.

The Lake House

Rose's maternal grandparents, Zoltan and Matilde Eordog, still lived in the small town of Szekszard, but had a house at the lake outside of town where they lived in the summer.

Trips to visit them at the lake were wonderful outings. At their end of the lake was a cove where older boys and young men loved to anchor their sailboats, creating a picturesque, idyllic scene. The Casino was always busy, being the favorite haunt of the older men.

The children would gather mushrooms and cook them. The family would pick up the kitchen table and set it in the lake where they would eat watermelon or their meals. One year Grandmother Matilde, who the children called "Nagymama," Grandmother, wrote a play, which the children acted out. She also made costumes for each of the characters. She had a deep love for Hungary, and everything she wrote was always patriotic. In this play, Rose was the Moon, wearing a silver and white dress with streamers representing the moon's rays and a headdress with shorter rays.

A young boy, whose father had died and whose mother worked long hours in a factory to support him and his brother, had attached himself to Paul and was carried by the family to the lake with the Takacs children. The Takacs parents always encouraged the children to include others in their activities. The warm acceptance the young boy, Rezso Lazar, received from the Takacs family affected him deeply. As an adult he moved to Canada, where he lives still and from where he still calls Rose frequently to talk.

Holidays

Christmas and New Year's were very special holidays for the family. The doctor would dress in his tuxedo, his wife in a long gown, the children in their finest. They would attend church, then have a festive dinner together. For New Year's, the dining table that could comfortably seat twelve people was covered with the finest foods: ham, salami, sausage, cheeses, cakes, bread, nuts, champagne, wine, and a Bible with money in it. These items represented what they desired to have in the upcoming year. There was salt, because it was good, but no vinegar or pepper because they didn't want to encounter angry people in the new year. Nothing sour or bitter. The table was laid out, but nothing could be touched until after midnight. By the time the clock struck twelve, appetites were well stimulated, and the feasting began.

The Good Doctor

No one died in Dr. Takacs's town if he could help it, as he carefully attended all who were sick, finding novel ways to treat and cure their ills when necessary. He paid for their medications when they were unable to do so themselves. He often went unpaid for his services.

He was truly a physician who wanted to help people, not one who sought wealth or prestige. On many nights, after the family was in bed, a knock would come on the door, and a neighbor would be there pleading, "Uncle Pal, please come and help my child." He quickly dressed and went. When a family member would question why he had to have his sleep disrupted so often, he would reply, "We can't let anybody suffer."

The family would often see him pacing up and down, up and down, pondering, trying to figure out how to treat a difficult illness. At the Medical Building where he worked, there were other doctors, as well. Many times there would be one patient waiting to see each of the other doctors, while there would be a long line outside "Uncle Pal's" door. The people knew it would be worth their wait. He treated all who came with the same consideration and kindness, regardless of their political leanings or ability to pay. He did this during the years Hungary was independent, when Nazi Germany took control, or when the Russian Communists ruled. Thus he sometimes had to treat Nazi or Russian soldiers. He treated them with as much regard as he did his fellow Hungarians.

Big Brothers

Rose's older brothers wanted to look out for their little sister, as older brothers do, of course. They said they wanted to help her become "resilient and tough, not stupid like other girls." This is evidently why they had her stand at rigid attention near the creek at the back of their yard while they put snakes or frogs down the front of her shirt. Part of their training for her required that she remain utterly silent while these creatures squirmed inside her shirt.

There are no poisonous snakes in Hungary, so her life wasn't in danger, but....

Also, as part of her training, to keep her from becoming vain, they told her frequently that she was ugly. "I can't bear to look at you," they would say, turning their heads away. This idea stuck, so she had trouble believing the comments made by artists when she was an adult that she was a classic beauty.

When she cried and ran to her father to complain about the brothers, he would ask, "Why do you play with them?" She always wanted to play with them, though, so each time, she went back for more.

Rose's brothers' training of her to be "resilient and tough" apparently worked, as she had an Appendectomy without anesthesia when she was a teenager. More on that later.

The brothers liked to fish in the creek and decided that throwing rocks from the railroad track that ran beside their yard into the creek would stir up the fish and make catching them easier. Friends would join in the rock throwing, and a good time was had by all until ... one friend threw a rock that accidentally struck Rose in the back of her head, making a big gash and causing profuse bleeding.

All of the children rushed Rose in to her father to tend the wound. The friend who had thrown the rock was terrified at what he had done. "Uncle Pal, I've ruined your daughter! I'm going to kill myself!" While the good doctor tended to her wound, which did not prove to be fatal, after all, this friend fixed his belt around a limb of a lilac tree and pretended to be ready to hang himself. He was only pretending and lived to see another day, as did Rose. She had lost a lot of blood, though, as it had run down her back and squished out of her shoes with every step.

As bad as this was, it actually was not the most dangerous situation Rose's brothers placed her in. One day she followed them up to the attic where they planned to lower her down to the ground through a window. The rope was only so long, so one brother stated, "We can't tie it around her waist because she's too fat, so we'd better tie it around her neck." Around the neck it went. They had her halfway out the window when their mother rushed in just in time to save her. She had heard the plotting downstairs and reached them just in time.

The children attended public school, did some homework in the afternoons (not too much), and played with the neighborhood children. They flew kites, played Hide-and-Seek, Tag, and other games that American children play.

Life was good and childhood all it should be until Rose was eight years old.

Chapter Five:
Troubled Times

Life would not remain comfortable and secure for this family, however, when new political upheaval occurred. Hungary's government chose a path that was not good for the citizens.

Hitler partitioned Czechoslovakia and gave part of Slovakia and all of Ruthenia to Hungary. Hungary withdrew from the League of Nations, and in 1939 signed the Anti-Comintern Pact with Germany, Italy, and Japan.

At the outbreak of World War II, Hungary claimed to be neutral, but the government was obviously in sympathy with Axis objectives. The Axis powers returned the northern portion of Transylvania to Hungary in 1940, and in 1941, Hungary sent troops into the territory awarded to Yugoslavia by the Treaty of Trianon and also declared war on the Soviet Union and the US. After suffering great losses in its army, Hungary approached the Allies for peace in 1943, causing Germany to turn on them and occupy the country. A puppet government was set up that began a reign of terror for dissidents and Jews, several hundred thousands of which were put to death or deported.[36]

World War II

So, Hungary had joined Germany in an invasion of Russia in 1941, but then Germany turned on its former ally and invaded Hungary after Hungary had approached the Allies for peace. The leaders of the country had aligned the country with Germany, but the populace was not in agreement with the Nazis. The Germans pressured Hungary to deport the Jews to German concentration camps, but Hungary refused to do so. This changed when Germany invaded and controlled

Hungary in 1943. "A total of 437, 402 Hungarian Jews were deported, most of whom were killed."[37]

To take territory from the Germans, Soviet troops now invaded and controlled the country by 1945.[38]

Russia began a fierce bombing campaign and sent in many ground troops.

Unfortunately, the Takacses' wonderful house with the wonderful yard was too close to the center of where the bombs were falling, so the family moved to an historic house that had been built many years before.

Takacses' Home[39]

On the first night in this house, the family had dinner, and when they had finished, Rose was helping her mother clear the dishes away and return them to the kitchen. Suddenly, sirens sounded and lights had to be turned out to avoid being the target of a bomb. With no light in the unfamiliar layout of the house, Rose made it to the hall but made a misstep and fell down the stairs. The dishes and scraps of food went in all directions. She was found unharmed but with a collection of radishes on her head.

In 1944, the house the family had moved from was destroyed by a bomb. If they hadn't moved the year before ....

Determined to live as normal a life as possible, in the yard of this second house, Dr. Takacs grew flowers that were the envy of all around. He cultivated Dahlias that were 12 to 15 inches in diameter, so that he was jokingly asked if he was using penicillin on them.

The Scourge of Communism

For a while, control of Hungary was passing back and forth between the Germans and the Russians, with fighting between the two militaries in the streets, placing the civilians in great danger. When Germany was in control there, the Allies dropped bombs, which often fell near the house. The Takacs family lived on one side of the Danube River, and on the other side was a group of factories producing munitions, the true target of the bombers. Many bombs fell on the wrong side of the river.

Close Call

One day in June of 1944, the doctor was coming home in his car, with bombs dropping all around. He had attempted to pick up Ferenc and Paul who were working in a factory, but when he arrived at their workplace, they had left for home, so he continued homeward. A bomb fell so close to the front of his car that it shattered his windshield. He arrived home covered in glass shards, but uninjured. Soon afterwards, the boys arrived, exhausted from running, crawling, and hiding, always seeking shelter, on their way home.

"A thousand shall fall at your side and ten thousand at your right hand, ..." (Ps. 91:7).[40] It came near, but not near enough to harm them.

Sometimes Dr. Takacs would send his family to the lake house of Rose's maternal grandparents, Zoltan and Matilde Eordogh, for safety for a while. The doctor, who was an officer in the reserves, had three or four Hungarian soldiers assigned to work with him, two of whom he sent to bring his family home after one stay at the lake. Rozsa had returned home in the morning of October 30, 1944. When the children were being carried home in the afternoon, bombs began dropping all around them, so the two soldiers pulled the four brothers and Rose out of the car and hid them on the hillside away from the approaching planes. Fortunately, they weren't spotted as the planes flew over, and they all reached home safely.

God was faithful: *"I will save your children"* (Isa. 49:25b).[41]

Zsolt remembers this vividly, as this day was his birthday. He remembers seeing many people walking on the road, and when he heard the planes, he expected to see the people being shot. This had happened frequently, but for some reason, not this time. He also remembers that he got a toy truck for his birthday that year.

Moving Again

After they were carpet-bombed in late 1944, the doctor knew it wasn't safe for his family to remain even in this, their second home.

Because life in and around the city was dangerous and nerve racking, the doctor's good friend who owned a champagne company was afraid to stay where the danger of being bombed was so great, so he re-located to a small village, where he remained till the end of the war. The champagne company was situated on a tremendous plot of land, totaling acres and acres, with a castle on the property being the home of the owner. The huge expanse also contained a park and a mausoleum. It was located away from the terrifying scene of street fighting and the bombing. The friend offered the doctor a small house that had been the home of the company manager. On a cold, snowy Christmas Day when bombs were falling all around, Dr. Takacs decided they couldn't remain a moment longer where the danger was so great and accepted his friend's offer.

Rose was nine years old. Since she had always wanted to play with her brothers, she had always wanted gifts like they had. This year was different. She had received her first doll. When the family hurriedly left the home, the doll had to be left behind with all the other Christmas gifts, including her first wristwatch.

Rose with Doll and Watch

They rushed to leave, taking nothing but absolute necessities, mainly warm clothes.

Zsolt, who was five years old, remembers being in his pajamas, playing with his train under the Christmas tree, then having to leave it behind.

The doctor gratefully moved his family into the champagne company Manager's house on this Christmas Day, 1944.

Tuberculosis Sanatorium

After three days of living in this small house, the Nuns who ran the nearby Tuberculosis Sanatorium asked the doctor to move his family into their facility and help take care of their patients. The Russians said the facility, which had been established for Postal Workers with TB, was not a true hospital since it had no male doctor, the male doctors all having fled in fear of the Russians. The Nuns explained that one of them was a doctor, but the Russians refused to accept her as such.

Dr. Takacs was glad to help, and feeling this would be an even safer place for his family, they moved into a small apartment in the TB Sanatorium. This had been the doorkeeper's space: one-bedroom, a kitchen, and a stairway to the root cellar. The children slept in the cellar, where the Nuns made beds for them, since this was the safest place because of the bombing from the Russians and other Allies that was incessant. Fear ruled the day, but in the cellar, the children were less frightened. The family felt this was God's provision for them.

The Russians stationed a cannon at the gate to the Sanatorium to guard against the Germans coming back. One of the Russian soldiers took a liking to five-year-old Zsolt, carrying him around on his shoulder. He would take him to the garden area of the Sanatorium and keep him on his shoulder while he took target practice. Zsolt's mother was, of course, terrified when this happened, fearful that Zsolt might be shot by accident. Still, she had no control over the Russian soldiers and could only pray for her child's protection.

One day the uncle of one of Zsolt's friends was playing with a hand grenade, spinning it around in his hand, with young Zsolt just 10 or 15 feet away. When the uncle was admonished that this was dangerous and he should stop, he boasted that he knew all about grenades and what they would or wouldn't do. About that time the grenade exploded, burning the uncle badly and sending shrapnel across the room into Zsolt. Many pieces were removed, but a piece that had lodged in the child's left hand remained there for many years. As a young adult, he claimed it as a badge of courage. It worked its way out after about 50 years, and Zsolt was actually a bit sad to lose it.

The damage to Zsolt could have been so much worse, as his mother certainly knew, but her family and her country were being controlled by a foreign power. She knew their only refuge was in God, to Whom she turned constantly in prayer.

Sirens would sound the alarm when bombs were in-coming, and Rose's family would duck under the table when they heard the warning. As terrifying as this was, when the sirens had been knocked out near the end of the war, everyone was more terrified because they had no warning.

Zsuzsy's Arrival

Rose's sister, Zsuzsanna (Zsuzsy), was born on January 6, 1945 in the Sanatorium a few days after the move. Rose remembers well the spectacular event that immediately preceded the birth. The table was set for the family to eat, with part of a ham that had been saved from the New Year's meal. Suddenly a bomb exploded nearby, creating a shock wave that sent the food into the air and against the ceiling, the ham hanging there in shreds. It looked like pulled pork. Within minutes, Zsuzsy was born.

Dr. Takacs had the newborn baby wrapped in a fur coat for warmth and was carrying her to the cellar where the children were staying for safety. Several Russian soldiers who were drunk were there, and one demanded of the doctor whether the fur was real or not. The doctor replied that it was not, but the drunken soldier demanded to have it. When the doctor didn't surrender it quickly enough, two of the soldiers pushed him down the ramp that led to the basement. Rolling over and over and sliding down the incline, the doctor protected the baby as well as he could, then handed over the coat.

There were ten wine cellars in the town, two champagne factories, and one hard-liquor distillery, all of which were available to the soldiers. The Russians were known to break the neck of a champagne bottle by striking it with a bayonet, and many were drunk all the time.

Soon Russia was completely in control of Hungary. Under Russian and later under the Hungarian Communist domination that followed, the nobility, the upper class, and many from the middle class were forced into labor camps. Many other men were forced into the Army.

Medical Ingenuity

One of the doctor's patients in the Sanatorium was a young man just 18 years old who had Tetanus. His muscles were already tightened, his jaws clamped shut, when he was brought to the doctor. Ordinarily, there would have been no hope for him, especially since there was no pharmacy from which to obtain any medication because of the war. The good doctor wouldn't give up on him, though. Dr. Takacs drew blood from several people who had been vaccinated against Tetanus and whose blood had antibodies against it, gave that blood to the young patient, and watched him recover. The young man's grateful mother was a florist, and thereafter, she sent the doctor's wife a bouquet of flowers every year to express her gratitude.

Before Russia gained complete control over Hungary in 1945, control over Budapest was changing hands almost daily between the German Nazis and the Russians, with incessant street-fighting. When soldiers were wounded and brought to Dr. Takacs for treatment, he wisely placed all German patients on the first floor of the hospital, the Russians on the second floor, and any Jews on the third floor, hoping none of them would discover the others.

Widespread Hunger

People were going hungry everywhere. When the doctor treated soldiers who needed him, they often brought him food as payment, since the military was being supplied with food. Rose's mother cooked everything that was brought and shared it with all who came hungry. Once the Russians brought a dead horse, which was quickly cooked and shared with those around who were in need. One day the Dean of the Catholic School came to the doctor's wife and asked if he could have just a cup of soup, he was so hungry. The Catholic and Protestant schools had now become the public schools, and priests and nuns were no longer wanted. When the church schools were nationalized, the priests and nuns who opposed this were tried and sentenced to life imprisonment, many being carted off to Siberia.

Rose's mother fed the Dean that day, of course, and continued thereafter when he needed it.

Mrs. Takacs prayed over and over, "God, the children must have food!" God was faithful. They always had more than enough so that they could share with others.

"You prepare a table before me in the presence of my enemies" (Psalm 23:5).[42]

Takacses' House

The Takacses' house, which they had been forced to vacate because of the danger, became the headquarters of the Russian soldiers. Dr. Takacs's Aunt Irma, now 82 years old, remained in the home, but came to the Sanatorium to eat with the family. One day she was frightened by the soldiers, so she escaped the house by climbing out of a window on a lower level and rushing to the Sanatorium. Generally, the soldiers were very respectful of the elderly and always treated her well.

The Takacses learned later that the Russian soldiers who now lived in their home were fascinated with many of its features. There were two toilets, complete with pull chains to use for flushing. Having never seen anything like this before, the soldiers thought the toilets were places to wash the face and head, and used them for that.

The soldiers had told Aunt Irma she couldn't go into the living room because there were government secrets there. They posted a sign stating this and sealed the door. When the war was over and the Russian soldiers had moved out, Dr. Takacs went to the government headquarters and asked about having the seal removed. A government official accompanied him back home to remove it, and the "government secrets" were revealed: the soldiers had stripped and taken the leather from a large leather sofa and two large leather chairs in this room. They had taken great care to prevent Aunt Irma from discovering this theft.

Gospodin Professor

One day in 1945, the Russian soldiers, who loved the doctor because he treated them with the same consideration he showed his Hungarian patients, brought him payment in the form of a tuxedo jacket, saying someone as distinguished as the good doctor should have a tuxedo. When the doctor looked inside, he saw his own name on the label. It was his tux, taken from his home, which Russian officers now occupied. The soldiers had not known it was his. In their admiration of him, they called him a "Gospodin Professor," saying someone as intelligent and educated as he, should be called "Professor," and they considered him saintly.

Yellow Star

As the doctor and his wife fed the hungry around them, they also fed a Jewish woman doctor, Dr. Safrany, and her two daughters, Ildiko and Sarolta, who had found a safe haven in the TB Sanatorium because both the Nazis and the Communists persecuted the Jews. Dr. Takacs had them stay in a small apartment in the back of the sanatorium, keeping out of sight as much as possible. The woman doctor was required by the Nazis to wear the yellow Jewish star on her shirt at all times, but Dr. Takacs had her wear a white lab coat over her clothes, so most people who saw her never knew she was Jewish. If any Nazis suspected she was Jewish and accused her of not obeying their command to wear the star, she could move her lab coat aside and show she was in compliance. Thus she and her daughters were spared from the concentration camps and probable death. Zsolt remembers her working on him to remove the shrapnel from the exploded grenade and seeing her lab coat fall open, revealing the yellow star.

> *Before World War II, about one in every twenty Hungarians was a Jew. But the Nazis and the Communists persecuted Jews until this number was reduced to about one in a hundred. ... Many Jews were killed or put in concentration camps.*[43]

One of Dr. Takacs's good friends, Dr. Adolf Kaldor, a fellow doctor who was Jewish, just disappeared with his family, presumably taken to a concentration camp for extermination. Dr. Takacs never heard anything of their fate.

Not only were the Jewish people in danger, but so were the Catholic Nuns and Priests if they objected at all to the changes the Communists were making. Dr. Takacs risked his own neck by putting lab coats on every one of them, disguising them as medical staff, though only one Nun was a doctor. His clever and courageous trick saved many lives.

Russia had gained complete control of the entire country by 1945.

Chapter Six:
Post World War II

The war ended in Hungary in late April of 1945.

Elections were held in November of 1945 with the Small Landholders' party winning over the Communist party, proclaiming a republic and installing a president. A coalition cabinet was formed between the Landholders and the Hungarian Communist party. Hungary was now on the verge of bankruptcy, there were shortages of food, prices were greatly inflated, and the transport systems were damaged. The Allies shipped in food to prevent starvation.[44]

The Allies, which included Russia, had won the war, and Russia, already in military control of Hungary, was now given official control. Rose says with dismay, "They gave us to the Russians." Therefore, a Communist government was formed, even though the Communists had come in second in the election. Russian soldiers remained and could be seen everywhere. Most Hungarians abhorred Communism.

Frugality

The Takacs family moved back into their house, but they now had to pay rent to the government, since it now owned everything. None of their personal possessions had survived the Russian occupation of the house. The doll, the wristwatch, Zsolt's train, nothing could be found.

Now they lived very frugally, as did the entire country under Communism, with the exception of those who rose to the top of the Communist Party. Members of the Communist Party who were in favor were given better clothes, more food, and better apartments. These bribes kept them loyal to the Communists.

Before this trouble began, Rose and her siblings were sometimes taken to concerts and operas that were geared to the interests of children, and they had clothes suitable for the occasion. Now, Rose had one blouse and one skirt which she wore every day to school. These had to be washed on Saturday, and if it happened to rain and the clothes didn't get dry, she couldn't go to church that Sunday. There were six children to clothe, so this was all the family could afford. Most people had very few clothes and had very little to eat. Rose says she feels her entire family lived in shock for a number of years.

Now the Allies shipped in food, and the Red Cross distributed it to the schools to feed the children of Hungary. One item shipped in large quantities was peanut butter, a substance not seen heretofore by these people. They wondered what it was, as peanuts are not grown in Hungary. Some speculated that it was pomade for the hair, and tried using it for that.

Totally Communist Government

In 1947, the leaders of the Small Landholders' party were arrested by the Communists, the legislature was dissolved and new elections held. The Communists won only 22 percent of the vote but dominated the coalition government that was formed. The Social Democratic party was coerced in 1948 into being amalgamated with the Communist party, forming the United Workers' party. In the new election in 1949, only communists were running. A new constitution was adopted, and the Hungarian People's Republic was formed.

Land was confiscated from peasants and turned into collective farms, and opponents to the Communist regime were sentenced to labor camps.[45]

By 1947 the government was totally Communist, and the new constitution that was adopted in 1949 was patterned on the Russian Communist Constitution.

No one could own private property. All homes and businesses belonged to the government. The owner of the champagne company was not only no longer its owner but had to leave Budapest, never to be allowed to return.

Communist Propaganda

Everything Russian was promoted: Russian books, Russian plays, Russian philosophy. Where Russia had the KGB, Hungary's Communist government had the AVH, Allam Vedelmi Hatosag, State Protecting Organization. These were Hungarians who spied on their fellow citizens, reporting any activity or statements that were critical of the government or Russia in any way. Within the AVH was a highly selected group called the AVO, Allam Vedelmi Osztag, State Protecting Special Group 17 who, because of their cruelty, were greatly feared by the populace.

The radio station had been taken over by the Communist government, and Communist propaganda was spewed daily. Anyone who worked there had to belong to the Communist Party. No longer was Hungarian music played, only Russian now. News and newspapers from the outside world disappeared.

Anyone suspected of being resistant to the Communist government could be hauled in for "re-education." This could consist of starvation and torture until the AVO determined the person was no longer resistant. If anyone criticized Russian equipment or dared to say they longed for their previous way of life, they could be hauled in and kept for weeks with no word to their families as to their condition. When they were released, they were afraid to speak of the treatment they had received while they were being held, fearing their family members might repeat the information and be picked up themselves. To get some extra food, because it was so scarce, any neighbor might turn you in if they overheard you speaking against the Communists. Words had to be guarded and thoughts kept to one's self.

The people were told that Capitalism was evil and needed to be abolished. Communism, on the other hand, would elevate the worker and bring everyone a better life. So they were told. In reality, the people could see that their economic condition was growing steadily worse and that they had lost all personal freedom.

Suspicion

In 1952, the Winter Olympics were held in Norway. A friend of the Takacs family, an Olympic athlete, brought Rose back an orange. No citrus grows in Hungary, so this was considered a delicacy, "imperialistic food," according to the Communists. Now the Takacses knew for sure their garbage was being examined in an effort to find incriminating evidence against the doctor, as they were asked about the orange peels. No international trade was allowed, so just how had orange peels come to be in their garbage? The AVO wanted to know.

The Lighter Side—Escapades

Both Protestant and Catholic classes had been held in the school, and these classes were allowed to continue for two years after the Communists took over. The children were to attend the one that matched their family's religion. While attending a religion class, the student skipped a standard education class. Zsolt attended both religion classes, pretending he was Catholic in one and Protestant in the other, until the school Principal spoke with his father. Well, the family did attend both churches, so ....

How much the ever-changing political climate affected Rose's character development, or how much was due to the inherited strong-willed character the entire family seemed to possess, is hard to tell, but Rose had an indomitable will. She says now, "I'm not too proud of myself." When she skipped school, she wrote her own excuses and signed her parents' names so cleverly even they couldn't tell the signatures were forged. One time she gave the school the excuse that the entire family had been quarantined for Scarlet Fever. Well, this had happened a few years earlier, so it wasn't entirely fictitious, she reasoned.

Stoic

One blaring example of her strong will stands out to show just how headstrong she was.

When Stalin died in March of 1953, Rose was 17. The Communist government ordered all of the school children to march in a parade to honor this cruel Russian. Rose started out with the group, but at the first street corner, she sat down on the curb, determined not to march a step further. When asked what was wrong, she quickly thought up an excuse and complained that her side hurt. She was taken to her father for examination. He thought she might have Appendicitis, and placed a thermometer in her mouth to see if she had a fever. When his back was turned, she agitated the thermometer to make the mercury rise and indicate a fever. Now convinced it truly was Appendicitis, he sent her to a friend who was a General Surgeon. This friend, who she called "Uncle Bundi," didn't want to take a chance on the appendix rupturing, so he quickly prepared to operate.

"I don't want to be put to sleep," Rose insisted. "But this will really hurt," the surgeon argued. Still Rose insisted, "Don't put me to sleep!" Finally, the doctor said "Alright," and began the totally unnecessary surgery. One would think that by now Rose would admit to the ruse rather than face such pain, but no. She lay perfectly still and said not a word as the surgeon cut open her side and removed the perfectly healthy appendix. Neither she nor the surgeon ever told her father that a healthy appendix was removed.

Trick

As teenagers and young adults, the Takacs boys and Rose were part of a group of 30 to 40 friends that "hung out" together all the time. They had parties and dances and generally spent all of their free time together, usually down near the Danube. Paul's girlfriend, Terezia, was part of the group, and so were Rose's best friend, Dalma, and her brothers. Afraid they were becoming a gang, an article was published calling them "houligans." The worst thing they ever did, however, was pull a harmless, humorous trick on a group of people. Zsolt and three or four others had heard of a trick they decided to try. They began looking up at the sky, exclaiming over what they supposedly were seeing, though there was nothing there. A crowd began to form. They continued to exclaim as before until about two hundred people had gathered around them. "Look how fast it moves!" "Look how shiny it is!" Finally some of the crowd began to say, "Oh, I see it now." Trick completed.

Medical Assistant

Since the Communist theory was that the Upper and Middle Classes had taken unfair advantage of the Lower Class, after High School Rose and her siblings were denied entry into the University because they belonged to a "privileged" class. The University was now reserved for the Lower Class, many of whom had no interest in a university education but rather desired a good job.

Rose managed to get a job in the Medical Building where her father worked. Because of her excellent work there, the authorities in the Medical Building insisted that the government allow her admission to College. Finally, she was admitted and obtained a two-year degree as a Medical Assistant. She continued to work in the Medical Building, drawing blood, doing EKGs, checking patients' vital signs, etc.

In 1953, after Stalin died, the government granted amnesties to some political prisoners and abolished internment camps, but Hungary joined the USSR and other Eastern European Communist countries in the Warsaw Pact for mutual defense and joined COMECON (Council for Mutual Economic Assistance).[46]

Chapter Seven:
The Hungarian Revolution

To the Communists, the Takacses were despised and held in suspicion. Since both were from aristocratic families and the doctor from a family of professional people, the groups the Communists declared had exploited the common people of the Lower Class, they were under suspicion and were continually spied upon. Also, the doctor had not joined the Communist Party and had continued his Christian activities, such as attending church. The Communist government kept track of who did this, and one friend of the family was fired from his job because he went to church. He was an official of the railroad, which was now owned by the government, and was the father of six or seven children. He was told he must stop attending church. He replied that his faith was important to him and that he could not fail to attend church. He was instantly fired.

Rose defiantly taught Sunday School one year.

The Doctor had to be allowed to have a telephone because people needed to be able to reach a doctor, but the family knew the phone was bugged and all conversations listened to.

They had known for years now that the Communists rummaged through the garbage, looking for incriminating evidence with which to accuse the doctor. Any mail that arrived had obviously been opened and often showed it had been greatly delayed before delivery. Words had to be very guarded because spies were everywhere.

By 1956, things reached critical mass. The Hungarian people had been suppressed and oppressed long enough.

The encyclopedia very concisely explained what happened this way:

> *On October 23, 1956, the Hungarian people began a revolution against the Communist regime. ... The Hungarian rebels gained control of most of the country ...*

> *but in November, Russian troops poured into the country to*
> *crush the revolt. The Russians set up a puppet government.*
> *... Many Hungarians were killed or sent to prison. About*
> *190,000 Hungarians fled to non-communist countries.*[47]

The rebellion was started by College and University students, demonstrating in sympathy with Polish students who had demonstrated for freedom and been jailed. High School students, including Zsolt Takacs, joined them, as did his two older brothers, Ferenc and Paul, and the next day, the whole country was in rebellion.

Weapons

As soon as the revolt started, the Hungarian soldiers who were housed in a downtown barracks opened the doors and gave guns and grenades to the rebels. These were soldiers the Communists thought would be loyal to them. Zsolt managed to get a Czechoslovakian machine gun and lots of ammunition, which he would use in the coming days. The soldiers in the barracks were advised by the rebels to take off their uniforms and leave, but many stayed and fought valiantly alongside of the rebels, showing they had been merely doing a job, but weren't loyal to the Communists at all.

During the days and nights of the revolt when Ferenc, Paul, and Zsolt were all out in town, their mother was constantly in tears, afraid they would be killed. She had tried to persuade them to remain at home, but to no avail. Now she prayed fervently for their safety.

Ferenc was asked to go to Austria to obtain medical supplies for the wounded rebels. A truck was provided with a driver, but an armed guard was also needed. Zsolt, armed with the Czech submachine gun, volunteered, and off they went. When they arrived at the Austrian border, the truck was allowed in with the driver and Ferenc, but Zsolt couldn't enter with his weapon. He stayed behind. At first he went to a school while he considered what he should do. There he decided he needed to get back to Budapest to see how he could further help. Fortunately, he was wearing a raincoat under which he could hide the gun when he needed to convince someone he wasn't involved in the rebellion.

Great numbers of Russian troops and tanks, sent in to put down the rebellion, amassed at the airport at the end of the main street in Budapest. Paul and Zsolt joined a group of rebels that had positioned themselves at the "S" curve through which the Russian troops and tanks would have to travel to reach the town. Some of the rebels had obtained some industrial grease, which they generously spread across the road at the "S" curve. Here Paul, Zsolt, and others waited for the tanks to slip and slide out of control, some landing in the ditch. From there the rebels fired on the Russians, and did their best to stop their advance into the city.

There was absolute mayhem on the streets during the rebellion. The rebels were shooting the AVO men when they found them. Looking through the window in his office at the Medical Building, Dr. Takacs could see the rebels stopping people on the street. When he saw them grab someone, knowing the captive could quickly be shot, Dr. Takacs would rush out into the street and tell the rebels, "No! Don't kill them! You don't want to do that! Let them go!" He was so respected by everyone that they obeyed him each time.

The rebels didn't shoot anyone in Budafok, which had been re-named District 22 by the Communists in 1950.

The great influence Dr. Takacs had would soon prove to be detrimental to his own wellbeing.

The rebels had control for only five days because they could not withstand the troops and tanks of the Russians that came pouring into the country.

Beautiful Budapest was damaged almost beyond recognition by the Russian tanks that went up and down the city's streets blasting buildings where it was suspected rebels might be hiding.

Hungary's Flag

The flag of Hungary is a horizontal tricolor of red, white, and green, these colors being Hungary's colors since the late 12th and early 13th centuries, and the flag's form remaining the same since the mid-15th century. Folklore attributes the colors to virtues: red for strength, white for faithfulness, and green for hope.[48]

Flag of Hungary

"The official Hungarian state flag does not contain the Hungarian coat of arms, but the coat of arms is often used during solemn occasions."[49]

Badge of Hungary[50]

This badge depicts the coat of arms of Hungary when it included Dalmatia, Slavonia, Bosnia, Flume, Transylvania, and Croatia.[51]

Note the cross at the top of the crown on the badge, depicting Hungary's establishment as a Christian nation around the year 1000.

Since Russia gained control of Hungary in 1945, "between 1946 and 1949 the crown was removed from the top of the arms serving as a badge."[52] The Communists would not recognize a crown and most certainly would not honor the cross, depicted at the top of the crown.

"In 1949, a new coat of arms featuring a Communist red star *[and hammer]* was placed on the flag as the badge."[53]

Badge with Communist Symbols[54]

"During the anti-Soviet uprising in 1956, revolutionaries cut out the Stalinist emblem and used the resulting tricolor with a hole in the middle as a symbol of the revolution."[55]

Revolutionaries' Flag 1956[56]

How symbolic was this flag, showing that Communism had created a hole in the very heart of Hungary. Except for those receiving special privileges from the Russian Communists, no one in Hungary wanted anything to do with the red star and hammer, and to see it on the flag of their beloved country was unbearable.

Current Coat of Arms of Hungary[57]

"The current coat of arms of Hungary was reinstated on July 3, 1990, after the end of communist rule."[58] The crown and cross returned, sometimes depicted with archangels upholding the badge from each side.

Chapter Eight:
The Bridge at Andau

James A. Michener wrote a very informative book, *The Bridge at Andau*, about the Hungarian rebellion, detailing the anguish felt by the Hungarians under Russian Communist rule, anguish that erupted into the revolution. Michener then told of the terrible aftermath of the rebellion.

Michener said, "Russia ... moved its brutal tanks against a defenseless population seeking escape from the terrors of communism, and destroyed it. A city whose only offense was that it sought a decent life was shot to pieces. ... A satellite country which had dared to question Russian domination was annihilated."[59]

Michener and other journalists had positioned themselves in Austria, just across the border from Hungary, near the small, nondescript bridge at Andau. From there they helped many frantic Hungarians cross into freedom. From personal stories of survivors, Michener pieced together a thorough description of all that had taken place with the rebellion, from its eruption among students on Oct. 23, 1956. Survivors who had escaped to Austria asked Michener not to reveal their names, saying, "If the secret police identify me in any way, they will kill my mother and father" who were still in Hungary.[60]

Of the bridge at Andau, Michener said, "Across its unsteady planks fled the soul of a nation. Across the bridge at Andau fled more than twenty thousand people who had known communism and who had rejected it. They had learned in sorrow that it was merely ancient terrorism in horrible new dress."[61]

The bridge did not connect Hungary and Austria but was entirely within Hungary. When one crossed it, one still had a few hundred yards to go to freedom. Andau, in Austria, was the closest village, and it received the fleeing Hungarians with open arms.

Rebels told Michener of their struggle for enough food and decent clothing under the Russian repression, even though they worked long hours (331 hours a month for the equivalent of $21 American dollars)[62] and attended the required indoctrination lectures extolling the glories of Communism. They told of goods they produced being sent to Russia, leaving none for Hungarian consumption, of having to always keep one's thoughts to one's self because spies were everywhere, and of fear of being spirited away for questioning and beatings without warning and without cause.

When the anguish reached critical mass among the students, they fearlessly attacked the radio station that spewed Russian Communist propaganda, the bookstores that no longer sold Hungarian literature but now only Russian propaganda, the Russian tanks that came against them, and the massive metal statue of Joseph Stalin that stood in the square where a church had previously stood. When the statue of Stalin was being pulled down, it broke off at the level of the top of his boots. Those empty boots were left there for their symbolic value.

When adults joined the students demonstrating in the streets, Russian soldiers machine-gunned hundreds, and when others tried to drag the wounded to safety, they were gunned down themselves.

The four-story barracks in town, mentioned earlier, housed the staff and soldiers that were appointed to the defense of Budapest. Michener said: "Of the four hundred communist soldiers in the barracks on the night of October 23—and they were men both trained and pampered by the Russians—not a single one remained faithful to communism."[63]

When the students rushed into the barracks asking for arms, the staff and soldiers handed out machine guns and ammunition, and then joined the fight on the side of the students. Here young Zsolt Takacs obtained the Czechoslovakian submachine gun and ammunition.

Young boys placed hand grenades in the paths of tank tracks, causing the tracks to be blown off and the tank to grind to a helpless stop. Students threw Molotov cocktails at the tanks, and when one student could get the door open into the tank, the cocktail thrown inside killed all of the soldiers within. Young children ran into the streets and thrust sticks inside the tracks of the tanks, causing them to stall. Such was the desire of all of the people to be free.

There were only a handful of Russian tanks in Budapest at the beginning of the rebellion. The soldiers inside one tank surrendered to the rebels, several tanks were destroyed, and some others retreated from the battle area. On November 29th, the Russians withdrew, giving the false hope to the beleaguered Hungarians that they had actually driven Russia away for good. "For five days Budapest delighted in the mistaken belief that Hungary was at last free of Russian domination and that some kind of more liberal government would replace the AVO terror."[64]

During the five days of quiet, newsmen from other countries swarmed into Budapest to learn what all had happened. The radio station that had not been allowed to play Hungarian music for years now played Mozart's Requiem Mass in honor of the hundreds of children, young students, and men and women who had died in the effort to secure freedom. The government jamming of outside radio news was lifted and news poured in from London, Paris, and Munich. Hungarians felt they were part of the world again.

Rose says, "We felt we were free at last! We thought our future would be free."

Then came ominous news: "A young boy came running into the streets crying that hundreds of Russian tanks were in motion at the airport. 'Not little ones like before. Big ones.'"[65]

"On Nov. 4th, Russian tanks stormed back into the city in force, imposing a worse terror than the AVO, and horribly crushing the revolution."[66] Russian tanks began tearing the city apart, blasting buildings up and down the city streets until they crumbled. "The glorious days of freedom were ended. The five brief days which had provided a glimpse into a different kind of future were over."[67]

Into Budapest came 4,000 Russian tanks, 2,000 being immediately employed, while the other 2,000 remained in reserve. Along with them came 140,000 of the most ruthless foot soldiers of the Russian army with orders to shoot, and shoot they did.[68] It didn't matter if the targets were small children or women standing in a line to obtain bread. The soldiers and tanks blasted away. They roared through the city, firing at random. Jet planes and propeller-driven bombers were called in to bomb certain areas, while rocket launchers were used to level whole buildings, killing all of the occupants. Flame throwers incinerated the inhabitants of large areas. Against all of this Russian power, the Hungarians had a few homemade gasoline bombs. "The time came ... on November 11, when further resistance was simply not possible."[69]

Radio

Voice of America and Radio Free Europe stations, encouraging freedom and democracy, had been secretly listened to by Hungarians. The Takacses listened, too, when the transmissions weren't being jammed. School children were questioned as to whether or not their parents were listening to these broadcasts, which were forbidden. The authorities would attempt to trick the children into confessions, asking "Which broadcast does your father listen to, the eight o'clock or the ten o'clock?" If the children innocently answered truthfully, the parents would be punished.

These broadcasts helped promote the rebellion. These secret listeners believed that as soon as those free people on the outside learned of their need for military help, they would rush in with arms and soldiers to assist the Freedom Fighters.

In the midst of the battle, a cry went forth to the world:

> From an unknown freedom radio station, an unknown fighter cried to the conscience of the world: "Civilized people of the world, on the watchtower of 1,000-year-old Hungary the last flames begin to go out. The Soviet army is attempting to crush our troubled hearts. Their tanks and guns are roaring over Hungarian soil. Our women, mothers and daughters are sitting in dread. They still have terrible memories of the Army's entry in 1945. Save our souls. S-O-S. S-O-S. People of the world, listen to our call. Help us––not with advice, not with words, but with action, with soldiers and arms. Please do not forget that this wild

attack of Bolshevism will not stop. You may be the next victim. Save us. S-O-S. S-O-S. ... Help. Help. Help. God be with you and with us."[70]

No help came from the outside world. Some say the broadcasts that made the Hungarians hunger for freedom simply incited the nation to commit suicide. Hungarians felt abandoned, and some felt bitterness toward the free world.

"After this there could be only silence."[71]

Toll

The freedom fighters tried to evaluate the damage done to Hungary. Eight thousand houses were destroyed with 60 percent of all the windows in Budapest shot out, 30,000 Hungarians were killed or wounded, with another 10,000 buried alive in collapsing buildings. Some Hungarians contested these numbers, saying the total of Hungarian casualties was actually 80,000.[72]

Propaganda

Now Russia began a propaganda program to convince the world that "the United States triggered the revolution and that it was participated in only by reactionaries ... and enemies of the working classes."[73] "We Soviets have intervened not as enemies but as true friends of the Hungarian people, and our own interest is only to help in putting down the revolt of fascists and criminal elements."[74]

The Strike

The propaganda might have worked with some, claiming that hot heads had revolted against the government without thinking, had the workers of Csepel, the ones coddled by the Communists, not joined the rebellion. They became part of the Freedom Fighters, joining the battle on every front. In one area that contained 15,000 workers, only 40 remained committed to the Communist government.[75]

When the rebellion failed in the face of tremendous Russian force, the situation was desperate for these workers.

On the afternoon of November 6, ... Russians began rounding up Hungarian men, tossing them into trucks, and carting them off to secret railway depots where they were herded into boxcars for shipment to perpetual slavery in Siberia. Possibly by plan, Russians allowed a few such deportees to escape so that news of this inhuman punishment could circulate throughout Hungary. To most Hungarians, such deportation to Siberia was truly worse than death, and many resisted it to the death, as their bullet-ridden bodies were later to testify.[76]

The Russians dominated the city, and through a puppet government made decisions of life and death. All food supplies were under Russian control, and only those Hungarians whom the Russians decided they could pacify were fed. The Russians also controlled the police, the health services and every operation of the city's existence. Anyone who dared oppose this Russian control ran the risk of starvation, imprisonment or execution.[77]

Would the workers bow down and be obedient to Russia's demands? Absolutely not! The workers called a strike on November 11th and continued it for months in spite of threats, false promises, and pleas. The men signed manifestoes and allowed themselves to be photographed, though they were sure these would later be used for retaliation. Michener said, "They were willing to stand forth undisguised and to demonstrate their contempt for their Soviet masters. I call that the ultimate in courage."[78]

That courage was not diminished when some of them braved the minefields to shepherd their families into Austria and freedom after it was obvious that continuing to resist was futile and their arrests were imminent.

Takacses Sons

This brings us to the 1956 story Zsolt told of his escape to Austria (see pages 6-12). He was actually in High School and not a University student as the newspaper article stated. At the time, he was 17, Paul was 24, and Ferenc was 26. The brothers had opposed the Communist regime and fired at the Russian soldiers. Now the revolution had failed, and soldiers were at the Takacses' house to arrest them.

Had Zsolt not spotted the soldiers when he did before going home, his story would have been very different. He would have been imprisoned and probably killed.

Paul was also in danger of being arrested or shot on sight. The Russian soldiers were shooting people without a trial, simply on the word of one person accusing them of having taken part in the rebellion and opposing the Communist Regime. Even little children were being shot in this manner. Hungary was enduring a nightmare of unbelievable proportions.

Paul, too, would have to flee to Austria for safety. Since Ferenc had not been allowed back across the border from Austria into Hungary, at this point his life was not in danger as were the lives of Zsolt and Paul.

University students came into Austria from the surrounding countries that were not Communist, hoping to help the Hungarian refugees in any way they could.

One student from Norway, Oystein, met Rose's best friend, Dalma, who had escaped to Austria, and took her back to Norway where his parents found her an apartment and helped her finish college. She had been a student at the Art Academy in Budapest. She and Oystein soon married, and she still lives there today. She and Rose have remained in contact through the years.

Dalma and Rose at High School Graduation[79]

Chapter Nine:
Paul Takacs

Young Paul Takacs, the second son of the Takacs family, had shown great artistic talent and would have attended the Academy of Applied Art in Budapest after High School, but the Communist regime in power was forbidding anyone from the "privileged classes" to attend the Universities. Allowing only the lower economic class to attend was the Communist idea of reparations, as their ideology stated those in the Upper and Middle classes had taken such unfair advantage of the poor.

Dr. Takacs had two close artist friends who tried to get young Paul the training his talent deserved, but were only able to get him into a school for Interior Design. There he designed furniture, though he had a talent for so much more, as he would later prove. Not being allowed into the Art Academy, he studied at private studios of painters and sculptors. Finally, because of the persistent intervention of the doctor's two artist friends, he was allowed to attend the Academy of Applied Arts of Budapest.

In October of 1956, he joined the rebels fighting the Communist regime with his girlfriend, Terezia, at his side. When their short-lived five-day victory was over, their lives were in danger. They had slipped into Terezia's home to tell her parents goodbye, leaving them bereft at the thought of possibly losing their only child. Then they hid in a peach orchard until dark and slipped unnoticed into the Takacses' home to tell Paul's mother and father that the two of them planned, under cover of darkness, to get aboard the train that would take them near the Austrian border. Only those with passports and visas could remain on the train to enter Austria safely, and since they would not have the necessary documents to officially enter, they would have to brave the minefield to get across the border.

His parents both wept, not knowing if the two young people would make it there alive, and not knowing if they would ever see them again. Still, they knew it wasn't safe for them to stay. Tearfully, they gave their blessing and kissed them goodbye. The parents did not know at this time what had happened to Zsolt, since he hadn't come home, and though they knew Ferenc had gone to Austria, they had heard no word on where he was. Now, with heavy hearts, they said goodbye to Paul and Terezia.

These two escaped just in time. The soldiers searched the Takacses' home, especially the attic, to see if the family was harboring one of the rebels or if guns were hidden there.

Safety

"Yea, though I walk through the valley of the shadow of death ... You are with me" (Psalm 23:4a).[80]

Paul and Terezia did make it out alive and found safety in a Refugee Camp in Austria. There wonderful things began to happen. Mrs. Jenny Strausser was the head of the International Travel Bureau in Vienna. She wanted to do something good for one of the many refugees flooding into her country from Hungary, so she went to the Refugee Camp to invite someone to come to her house for the day, to enjoy some creature comforts not available in the camp and to be richly fed. She picked Paul. She and Paul could only communicate with gestures, since they spoke different languages, but the visit was a very welcome gift to him.

The next week when Jenny Strausser went back to the camp, she couldn't find Paul, but found Terezia and took her home instead, not knowing she and Paul were together. She soon learned they were a pair and became attached to both of them, bringing both to her house again and again. Since the Takacses back in Budapest had a phone, at Christmas Jenny Strausser called to let Paul's parents know that he and Terezia were safe and where they were. In February of 1957, she helped them get married at her house, filled the refrigerator with food, told the young couple to use her house as their Honeymoon Suite, and left for a trip with her daughter. Zsolt, who was in the same refugee camp, was able to attend the wedding.

Wedding of Terezia and Paul[81]
Zsolt, Terezia, Jenny Strausser, Paul

If the Takacs sons contacted their parents, their parents would be punished by the Communists. So Jenny traveled to Budapest to see the Takacs family and offered to be a "bridge" for communication between them and their young refugees in her country. When Rose asked her why she was being so caring and generous with Hungarian refugees, she told the family her story.

Living in Vienna with her husband and young daughter during World War II, this Jewish family was in grave danger when the Nazis began rounding up Jews in Austria and shipping them to death camps. They managed to escape to Switzerland, where a wealthy family successfully hid them until the end of the war, risking their own lives to do so. The Straussers returned to Vienna at the end of the war where Jenny's husband, Peter, soon became Prime Minister. They made a trip back to Switzerland, hoping to reward with money the brave family for saving their lives. The Swiss family thanked them for the thought, but said they had no need of money and were happy they had been able to help. Now Jenny made a vow: "If I ever see someone in need, I will do all I can to help them." Jenny felt very gratified to have been able to help Paul and Terezia, and wanted to continue to help the family in any way she could.

What a wonderful, selfless person Jenny Strausser was! Her husband had left her for a Hungarian refugee woman, yet she did all she could for Hungarian refugees. The Takacses saw her as a wonderful God connection.

America, France, Canada, and Australia opened wide their arms to receive Hungarian refugees. Those coming to America were sent first to Camp Kilmer, New Jersey.

After three months, as soon as all the official hurdles could be cleared, Paul and Terezia were sent to the United States. They arrived at Camp Kilmer, New Jersey with only $10 from the International Rescue Committee, speaking no English.

Paul Takacs, the Artist

A Hungarian woman in Washington, DC who was working with the refugees at Camp Kilmer by finding work for them, found young Paul a job in Washington as a draftsman, creating renderings for architects. All he needed was a chance, and he was on his way. After one week, he was hired permanently and remained at that job for seven years before beginning to free lance.

He and Terezia settled in Silver Spring, MD, where he would become a famous artist and sculptor, classed as a "Renaissance Artist" by some.

Terezia had also attended the Art Academy in Budapest and was an excellent artist in her own right. She became an illustrator at the Smithsonian Institution, doing textile design, painting, and designing small ceramics. The two of them taught themselves English with the help of newspapers and a dictionary.

Paul's first painting in the US was "Broken Hearts," painted in 1957, displayed below and on the cover of this book.

Broken Hearts[82]

The photo depicts the Hungarian family, walled-in and unable to enjoy the bright, blue, wonderful world of freedom just beyond their reach.

Here's what Paul said about the painting.

My first painting in the U.S.A.! I was going to send it to Vienna, (Austria) to participate in a commemorative show of the Hungarian Revolution. To protect my family—in my fear—I painted over my name!

The show could not be held because the Russians threatened the Austrian Govt!—To remind myself, how afraid we have been—I left my name painted over.

—At the end of 1957 my Father was taken away in the middle of the night, our home was turned inside-out!—After a long time of uncertainty, they produced a trial, (closed) where my Father—for bringing up his sons as enemys of the state—

was sentenced to life in prison, (death was asked) suffered six long years!

> broken hearts ...
> Paul Takacs[83]

In 1964, Paul made a trip to Vienna, Austria, since he couldn't enter Hungary, to see his mother for the first time since the tearful parting in 1956. Dr. Takacs had served those six years in prison and had been released the year before, but the Communist government would not give him a passport to come to Austria. They said that since he had been a political prisoner, he might defect if he were allowed to leave the country. If Paul entered Hungary, he would be arrested, and he might be hanged, so he only got to see his mother and Rose, along with Jenny Strausser, at whose house they stayed for several days.

Paul with Rose, Jenny Strausser, and Mother Rozsa in Vienna[84]

Jenny visited the Takacs family in Budapest after Dr. Takacs was released, and she visited Paul and Terezia in the US almost every year until her death.

Exhibitions and Honors

Paul's first one-man show was sponsored by the American-Hungarian Cultural Center.

His works were placed on exhibit at the Hungarian National Gallery in November of 1990. Here are the remarks given by the Art Historian, Gabor Odon Pogany.

It is a great pleasure to all of us that a student of the Hungarian University of Applied Arts, Interior Design, has now returned to us, as a master, as an honorable artist. This rich collection presents the most interesting features of his art from the past 30 years. However, I must tell you that this collection, as characteristic as it is, is incomplete. The artistic oeuvre of Pal Takacs is much richer, much more arborescent, because he is something like a general factotum of art. I have to say that he is a natural talent, who makes use of and represents the original potential of art, which is successful in the creation of any kind of art. He belongs to that great line of Renaissance artists who were painters, sculptors, and architects at the same time. He is as good as an interior or exhibition designer as he is as creator of large-scale sculptures and graphics, small, intimate panel paintings, or monumental creations. I regret that we have no chance to see the grand monograph dealing with his art. I have seen a few documentary pictures showing the wide range of his creations: wall pictures, metal reliefs, remarkably interesting, dynamic, large and small metal sculptures. He is equally at home in the intimate genre as in monumental versions because he creates medals and graphics as well. His graphical activity is especially appealing. I have to say that as a graphic artist he has proved his ability to pursue all kinds of fine art, because, as Michelangelo said, drawing is the basis and origin of all arts. Besides his greater paintings and compositions, observe the smaller drawings. See that creative activity, almost as easy flowing as handwriting, which is Pal Takacs's personal style, the unique source of his art. ... And that is what I consider very important in his art: it is human, it has a positive effect on mankind. I wish him success and further manifold, arborescent creative work.[85]

Paul had many exhibitions, and his artwork hangs in the Albertina Museum, Vienna Austria; Peabody Museum, Nashville, TN; Evansville Museum of Art and Sciences, Evansville, IN; Laura Musser Art Gallery & Museum, Muskotin, IO; Sheldon Swope Art Gallery, Terre Haute, IN; Washington County Museum, Hagerstown, MD; National Air and Space Museum, Washington, D.C.; Arts and Industries Museum, Washington, D.C.; and in various private collections throughout the world.[86]

Paul's Drypoint Etching of the face of Moses with the tablets of the Ten Commandments super-imposed over it hangs in the Albetina Museum in Vienna, Austria,[87] and a copy hangs in the Cumner Museum of Art in Jacksonville, FL, donated by Zsolt.

Moses (Drypoint Etching)[88]

In 1990, Paul won the American Numismatic Association Centennial Medal Design Competition, and in 1991, he won the City of Historic Laurel Mural Competition.[89]

Colonel Kovats Sculpture

Paul has murals and sculptures in many places, including the life-size sculpture of Colonel Michael Kovats de Fabricy on horseback which stands in front of the Hungarian Embassy in Washington, D.C. The following information is taken from a booklet given to those attending the dedication ceremony for the unveiling of the statue. The information was compiled by Dr. Elemer Bako.

Colonel Commandant Kovats, a Hungarian, is considered the Father of America's Cavalry, having come to America in 1777.

He had fought in a Hussar regiment for Hungary, fought for a French king, then for a Prussian king, always fighting for freedom, and for a time served as a courier to the French court for Poland. The American Declaration of Independence resonated with his willingness to sacrifice all for any people to be free, so he wrote Benjamin Franklin asking for a recommendation to Congress so that he might serve America's cause of freedom.

After he received Franklin's recommendation, the Polish Brigadier General Pulaski convinced George Washington that America needed a cavalry, and he recommended Kovats to develop it. Washington agreed, and in March of 1778, the Pulaski Legion was sanctioned with Kovats as Colonel in command. He fought valiantly for America against the British, and when he was killed in battle in Charleston, SC in 1779, he became the first Hungarian who sacrificed his life in the service of the United States of America.[90]

Paul had a great appreciation for the freedom America had granted to him, so he also had a great appreciation for the contribution of his fellow-countryman, Kovats. In the early 1970s, Paul created a clay model from which the present bronze statue was cast. The statue depicts Kovats and his horse in the throes of death as both had been shot and were collapsing. Even as he was dying, Kovats held high the American flag, demonstrating the motto the society named for Kovats had chosen to represent him: "Fidelissimus ad Mortem," "Most Faithful Unto Death."

"Fidelissimus ad Mortem," "Most Faithful Unto Death."[91]

The statue was placed at the Hungarian Embassy and dedicated on October 11, 2003, with members of the First California Hussar Regiment in their circa 1848 Hungarian Hussar uniforms in attendance. Smaller models in bronze were given to family members.

First California Hussar Regiment

Zsolt, Rose, Ferenc (Frank)

Scholarship

After Paul's death on August 22, 2000, his wife, Terezia, put together a Sketch Book of his paintings and sculptures in his memory. The book is presented to the recipients of the scholarship established in his name at the Academy of Applied Art of Budapest, Hungary.

Below are some paintings included in the Sketch Book.

Terezia[92]　　　　　Self Portrait[93]

Paul and Terezia have two daughters, Rozsa Jenny and Terezia Ildiko.

Paul's Children[94]

Paul's Parents[95]

Jenny, 1960[96]

Chapter Ten:
Zsolt Takacs

Back to Zsolt's escape.

There were Guard Towers every ten meters along the border where there was no barbed wire. The guards were armed and quick to shoot. Zsolt didn't run into any barbed wire, but he knew the Guard Towers were there and that the danger was great. As he indicated in his newspaper article printed on pages six through twelve, he had indeed crossed over into Austria and circled back into Hungary without knowing it.

After he was captured by Hungarian soldiers loyal to the Communist government and then rescued by the small band of Freedom Fighters, Zsolt finally crossed the border at Mosendorf, Austria in the dark where all he could see was an occasional shadow. Austria had Guard Stands dotted along the border, too, and Zsolt heard "Halt! Are you carrying any weapons?" spoken in Hungarian with an accent. The guards were not there to keep the fleeing refugees out, but helped them get safely to freedom.

Zsolt helped a woman with two children get across. As soon as he realized he was on Austrian soil, he dropped to his knees and gave thanks.

By this time, he hadn't eaten in many hours and felt starved. CARITAS, the Catholic Relief Agency, was prepared to feed the refugees with chocolate milk and cheese. Over and over, Zsolt was fed chocolate milk, bread, and cheese, which he and the other refugees began to refer to as "CARITAS cheese." While they would have preferred some variety, they were grateful for any food at all and ate it without voicing complaint.

Detained

The thousands of refugees that were pouring over the border into Austria were carried by bus to various locations where they could be housed. Zsolt was taken to Salzbourg to Camp Roeder. Just as Jenny Strausser befriended Paul and Terezia in the Refugee Camp at Vienna, citizens living near the camp where Zsolt was placed invited some of the refugees into their homes for the Christmas holidays.

Zsolt found himself invited into the home of a family who had him spend Christmas with them in the Swiss Alps where they owned a resort hotel. He even got to visit the little chapel where Franz Gruber gave the first performance of "Stille Nacht," "Silent Night." Gruber had written the music to Joseph Mohr's poem and shared it with the members of the little chapel on Christmas Eve a hundred years earlier. What a Christmas celebration for a refugee who had just suffered the agonies of war and defeat!

The family into whose home he had been invited wanted to keep him. They said he could go to the University of Heidelberg and "become somebody, a doctor, maybe." They allowed the other refugees to go back to the camp, but detained Zsolt for two extra weeks, thinking he would make a good husband for their daughter, whose appearance Zsolt describes as "unfortunate." He did not want to stay.

Since Ferenc had crossed the border to obtain medical supplies and had not slipped in as a refugee, he wasn't being housed in a refugee camp. Somehow either he or Paul got wind of the fact that Zsolt was being held by this family, so they sought for help to get him released.

Now Jenny Strausser came to his rescue, befriending him just as she had Paul and Terezia. As the ex-wife of the Prime Minister of Austria, she had enough influence to affect a change. At her insistence, apparently Peter Strausser himself ordered the family to release Zsolt and deliver him to the camp in Vienna where Paul was.

Australia or America?

Zsolt was soon given a ticket to be settled in Australia, along with a friend he had known in Budapest. Zsolt talked with Paul and several old friends in the refugee camp who convinced him he should come to America with them. What could he do, since he was officially assigned to travel to Australia? He asked for a change, but was told "No."

Now Jenny Strausser came to his rescue again, and Peter Strausser ordered Zsolt's assignment to be changed to Putney, Vermont, though the quota for Putney had already been filled. Willie Spitz, an Austrian government official, had picked the ten to go to Putney, but was persuaded to override the limit and include Zsolt. America would be Zsolt's new country.

Ference, Paul, and Zsolt talked and agreed that Ferenc would go to Canada and the other two would go to America. They would see which country offered the best prospects for the future, then the three would locate there. As it happened, Ferenc found he loved Canada, and Paul and Zsolt loved America, so they each stayed put.

Zsolt and other refugees were loaded onto an old Navy plane, which landed first in Shannon, Ireland to refuel. There he and his fellow refugees were treated to an absolute feast. In the middle of the table loaded with food was a dish with little yellow balls piled high into a pyramid. He and the others speculated about what those little balls could possibly be, since they had never seen any food shaped in this way. Finally one of his friends volunteered to brave tasting one of the yellow balls on behalf of the whole group. He put one on his plate and carefully sliced it into thin slices, then cautiously put it into his mouth. Butter! It was simply butter that had caused so much consternation!

America

From Ireland they went to Nova Scotia, Canada, then on to Newark, New Jersey and Camp Kilmer, landing on March 7, 1957. There were thousands of Hungarian refugees in the camp, and they all were put to work doing the jobs that had to be done to take care of such needs. Just as in the military, some peeled potatoes, some cooked, some cleaned. Jobs were rotated, so Zsolt got to experience a variety of labors. So relieved to have gained freedom, the refugees were happy to do all they could to avoid being a burden.

The refugees had only been interviewed while in Austria, not closely questioned. Now they were interrogated over and over to be sure they had no plans to do harm to their host country.

Zsolt's final stop was Putney, Vermont. While in Vermont, Zsolt attempted to get in touch with his parents to assure them once again that he was safe and to let them know his whereabouts. A strange woman answered the phone instead of one of his family members. When she began to pump him for information, he quickly hung up. He realized the call had been intercepted and could mean dire consequences for his parents. His family in Hungary was still very much endangered, and he didn't want to give the Communists more ammunition to use against them.

His life, on the other hand, was going extremely well. In Putney, he found himself fortunate enough to be included in a program called "Experiment in International Living," the Student Exchange Program, lead by Dr. Jack Wallace. The program had enlisted a number of outstanding citizens, such as politicians and university professors, to host these refugees in their homes.

Zsolt found himself placed in the home of Dr. Steve Blickenstaf, who was on sabbatical from his job as professor at Columbia University, and so was at his home in Vermont. Dr. Blickenstaf later left his employment at Columbia University to become the head Accountant for the Experiment, a program that still provides for a period of life abroad for Exchange Students. The motto of this program is: "Walk together, talk together, all ye people of the earth," thereby promoting understanding and cooperation among all nations.

The young refugees in this experimental program led by Dr. Wallace met each morning at Dr. Wallace's house to learn English. Dr. Wallace had a beautiful flower garden to which they retired for lunch. They had each come from their host homes bringing their lunch. When they had been asked what they would like to eat, they all had politely responded, "Anything's okay. Whatever you want to send." Big mistake.

They each came bringing peanut butter and jelly sandwiches. The host families knew these to be popular among American children, so they assumed it would be the same story for these young men. In truth, peanut butter was a strange food indeed to these guys. As was mentioned earlier, peanuts are not grown in Hungary, and peanut butter is not eaten. Day after day the host families sent this same fare, believing that the boys were enjoying it because, when asked if lunch was good, the boys all politely said, "Wonderful."

If peanut butter and jelly sandwiches could grow, Dr. Wallace would have had an enormous new crop in his garden.

Soccer

Dr. Wallace asked one day, "What do Hungarian boys like to do?" He was told they liked to play soccer, so they were given a soccer ball. Zsolt had actually played on a Youth League team while growing up in Hungary, as had the goalie, Tom Illes. Of the eleven young refugees, eight were from Budafok, and all but one had played soccer with neighboring boys day after day in their free time. Zsolt remembers that they would go play in front of the school. Knowing that the girls would be looking out the windows at them, they often took off their shirts to show off for the observers. Now they made a good team with a tight bond forged in the fire of the revolution.

Soon they were allowed to play the soccer team at nearby Wyndham College. When the famous Tottingham Hot Spur from Tottingham, England came to tour the US and play college teams, Dr. Wallace persuaded them to also play his Hungarian refugee players.

The refugees had no uniforms, so Zsolt volunteered to sew uniforms for them if Dr. Wallace would purchase the material. Zsolt had no experience at sewing, other than watching someone sew clothes for the family during his childhood, but he did it. He sewed uniform pants for the team's eleven players. Now they were given white t-shirts with numbers written on them with Magic Markers. Next came the problem of shoes, so they were taken into town to the local shoe store. Predictably, the store had no soccer shoes, so they were given tennis shoes. Now they were ready to meet the Tottingham Hot Spurs.

When the Hot Spurs' bus arrived, out stepped the women who were accompanying the team—decked out in loads of furs and diamonds—

then the well-uniformed Hot Spurs. The Hungarian refugees in Zsolt-sewn pants and Magic Marker t-shirts with tennis shoes beat Tottingham's famous team three-to-two. Stunned and chagrinned, the Hot Spurs left. Two weeks later, Dr. Wallace received a call from the team's manager asking for a re-match. The loss was a fluke, the manager was sure, but the team couldn't allow such a record to stand.

Before the re-match, the Hungarians were carried to Boston to buy the proper shoes. This game was played with the same uniform, but this time with soccer shoes. Hungarians four, Hot Spurs three. No further re-matches were requested. Tom Illes, the goalie, was a stellar player and was given credit for winning the games for the refugees.

Years later Zsolt found himself in London and asked to see the record of the games played when the Hot Spurs toured America. He was told the Hot Spurs only played in California when they were in the US. That was the official story. No admission that a rag-tag bunch of refugees had beaten England's superstars.

Zsolt was enrolled in the Vermont Academy where he earned a High School diploma. He and the other Hungarians were taken to visit a number of colleges to encourage them to pursue higher education. Zsolt was granted a full scholarship at the University of Delaware, but only took advantage of this opportunity for one year.

The Hungarian refugees receiving diplomas in
Putney, Vermont. Zsolt is first on the left.

Divine Protection

To look at all of the near tragedies he had survived, to see all of the privileges afforded him, some people would say Zsolt had lived a "charmed" life.

For the family to have moved from their home the year before it was bombed,

To have not been killed or severely maimed by the shrapnel when he was five and the grenade exploded,

To have been protected during the massive bombing by the Allies,

To have escaped being shot during the days and nights of the rebellion,

To have spotted the danger awaiting him at his home while he was far enough away not to be seen and caught,

To have been allowed to travel by rail close enough to the Austrian border to make it to freedom,

To have escaped being shot by the guards in the guard towers dotting the border,

To have avoided stepping on a mine when he couldn't see anything in the pitch-black dark,

To have travelled safely through the minefield twice,

To have been rescued by a band of Freedom Fighters when he was being sent by truck back into Hungary to sure imprisonment or death,

To have found safety in a refugee camp,

To have been carried by a host family to the Swiss Alps for Christmas and to the chapel where Silent Night had first been performed,

To have found his brothers while in the Refugee Camp,

To have been allowed to change his destination from Australia and come to America,

To have found himself living in the home of a university professor,

To be a part of Dr. Wallace's Student Exchange program,

To be taught English,

To attend Vermont Academy free,

To receive a full college scholarship ...

All just happenstance? Coincidences? Far from being typical for refugees, all of these experiences were clear indications of Zsolt's life being orchestrated by an all-powerful, all-knowing, loving, divine being. Zsolt says, "You trying to tell me I just lucked out?"

He gives all credit to the loving care of Almighty God Who answered the prayers of his praying mother, who he refers to as an angel personified, and the God Who honored the integrity and sacrifices of his father.

"For you have been a shelter for me, a strong tower from the enemy" (Ps. 61:3).[97]

After five years in America, Zsolt made the trip to Vienna to meet with Rose that he mentioned in the newspaper story. He wouldn't see his parents until 1969 when they came to America for a visit. There was still a Communist government in Hungary, and as a rebel, he was persona non grata. He still could have been imprisoned or killed had he dared enter the country.

Marriage

While in Putney, Vermont, a young woman whose mother worked for Dr. Wallace's Experiment in International Living came to visit. She had been living in St. Louis, Missouri with her father. Nancy and Zsolt got to know each other, soon married, and had three children: Victoria, Kathlyn, and Thomas. Years later when this marriage ended in divorce, Zsolt moved to Paul and Terezia's in Silver Spring, Maryland.

He soon opened an Employment Agency in Silver Spring, but gave it up to become the manager of the cafeteria of the Capitol Democrat Club. There he did an outstanding job of procuring the foods and other items needed for the restaurant, earning the gratitude of the owners who wanted to promote him. He told the restaurant owners that if they ever had a job opportunity in Florida, he would consider it.

Ruthie

Next door to Paul and Terezia's was a family with eight children. The mother was French, and the father, though an American citizen and a valuable member of the US Army, was Greek. During World War II, he earned five Bronze Stars for his outstanding contribution to the American war effort. When someone was needed to penetrate the enemy lines and gain military information, Eisenhower often said, "Get the Greek," meaning, of course, Louis Eliopulos. His fluency in five languages was very valuable, and his courage made him a tremendous asset for America. He was an authentic hero.

As much as Zsolt liked and admired the entire family, his special interest was the beautiful daughter, Ruthie. As "the girl next door," she had won his heart, and in 1972 they married. They had three children: Zsolt, Aniko, and Kristina. Later, Zsolt and Ruthie carried these children to Budapest to be christened in the Reformed Presbyterian Church in which he had grown up.

Zsolt, Attila's daughter Aniko, Niki, Tina, Zsolt, Jr., Attila's son Attila, Ruthie[98]

Jacksonville, FL

Now Zsolt's employers procured a contract for a restaurant in Jacksonville, Florida and offered him the chance to move to the place he was most interested in. As soon as he and Ruthie were settled in Jacksonville, his employers lost the contract and told him he would need to move to Atlanta. Florida was his goal, so he turned down their offer, leaving himself without a job.

Ruthie's father owned a number of cemeteries and purchased Restlawn Cemetery in Jacksonville, asking Zsolt to run it for him. Restlawn had been an "all white" cemetery, the contract specifying "Caucasians only."

Zsolt and his father-in-law felt such discrimination was repugnant and opened it for all races. Zsolt was stunned at the anger this stirred up, bringing death threats. He and his family lived across the street from the cemetery, so they were very vulnerable. For a month, until things calmed down a bit, he slept with a gun under his pillow. For his open and fair-minded attitude, grateful black families brought him cookies and ice cream, and lots of business.

His father-in-law also owned the Jacksonville Suns baseball team, making Zsolt the head of Security for members of the Press in the

Press Box. Everybody wanted to get in to speak to members of the Press, but Zsolt was their protector, guarding the door.

Zsolt soon heard that Edgewood Cemetery was for sale. It had been open since the Civil War, handling about 85 burials per year. As soon as word got around that Zsolt had bought it and that any race was welcome, business boomed, going from the previous 85 burials per year to over 600 the first year. He later bought a cemetery in West Palm Beach, and one at Jacksonville Beach, FL.

BS Degree, Cum Laude

When all six of Zsolt's children had graduated from college, they challenged him that he needed to complete his education. He had completed only one year at the University of Delaware, though he had been given a scholarship for a free and complete college education. He had chosen to go to work instead. Now in his 50s, he decided it was his time. While continuing to work, he studied hard, taking evening classes, and graduated Cum Laude from LaSalle University in three and a half years with a Bachelor's Degree in Business. His thesis was entitled *"Hungary's Movement Toward a Market-Based Economy After the Collapse of Communism,"* reflecting his love for his native country. He concluded his thesis with the Latin phrase *"Dum Spiro, Spero,"* "As long as I breathe, I hope."[99]

Official Visit to Hungary

Included in his thesis was information concerning his involvement in a high level financial delegation to Hungary, sponsored by Morgan Stanley in 1994. Russia had left in 1991, and Communist domination of Hungary had finally ended in 1992. To recover from the harm Communism's central planning had caused, Hungary would need a lot of foreign investment.

Travelling in this delegation with the American Ambassador to Hungary as a consultant to Morgan Stanley, Zsolt's access to the highest levels of government in Hungary was very valuable in introducing investors to those government officials. In 1993, Zsolt had declined a request from this US Ambassador to Hungary that he become the American Commercial Attache to Budapest.

Zsolt's mother was still living at this time, so Zsolt took the Ambassador, Marc Palmer, with him to visit her. Attila and others had tried unsuccessfully for years to get the government to pave the road leading to the house, which became an almost impassible, muddy mess when it rained.

Zsolt pointed out to the local officials how bad it looked to be taking the Ambassador over such a muddy, slippery mess of a road. The road was quickly paved.

"Apu" and "YaYa"

Today, Zsolt has six children, 18 grandchildren, and four great-grandchildren, with another on the way. He and Ruthie pick up three of the grandchildren after school, help with homework, and feed them dinner before sending them home when the parents are through with their workday. To his grandchildren, Zsolt is "Apu," Hungarian for "Daddy." Ruthie is "YaYa," Greek for "Grandmother."

Ruthie and Zsolt

Zsolt says that the fact that a refugee coming to America in 1957 speaking no English, could have the very successful business career that he has had "can surely demonstrate that the American Dream is still possible with the help of God, family, and hard work!"

Chapter Eleven: Prison

Arrest

In 1957, shortly after the Revolution, Dr. Takacs was arrested. The charges were that he had "raised his sons to be enemies of the state." Also, he had continued his Christian life in spite of the Communist government, and the Communists felt he had too much influence with the local people. He couldn't be allowed to sway others away from Communist ideology.

Dr. Pal Takacs

He had suffered a heart attack in January of 1957, had been in the hospital for a while then discharged, but sent to the Sanatorium to recuperate. He had been in the Sanatorium for one month when the soldiers came and arrested him in May. He had suffered a previous heart attack in his 30s. Now at age 57, weak with this life-threatening illness, he was heartlessly thrown into jail.

About a week after he was arrested, a Communist Hungarian police officer called Rose in for a "talk." He told Rose, "Your father could be out of prison in 24 hours if you would be my mistress." Rose replied, "I think my father would rather die in prison than to have me do such a thing, and I would rather he stay there and die than do what you suggest." Then the police officer threatened, "Then we're going to wipe out every trace of your family. You'll all be gone." To this Rose replied, "I know you have the power to do it. Do it quickly then. Hurry up."

Courage

Many years later, one of Zsolt's friends who had been arrested at the same time Dr. Takacs was, related a story the doctor had never, and would never, tell his family. The friend told of being in a holding cell with the doctor and a number of young students after the rebellion. Dr. Takacs, called "Uncle Pal" by this group as he was by everyone, told the young men: "You are young and have your whole lives before you. I'm older. Tell them everything was my fault. Blame everything on me, and maybe you can go free."

"Courage (kur'ij) n. That quality of mind or spirit enabling one to meet danger or opposition with fearlessness."[100] It should also read: "That quality exemplified by Dr. Pal Takacs."

As the Doctor was being interrogated, he was accused of things that had been spoken in his house that the authorities had no way of knowing unless the house was bugged. There had been no one there except the family when these conversations took place, yet the authorities knew exactly what had been said. The Communist government had had the opportunity to bug the house when the Russians occupied it back in 1944 and 45. The family had known they were targeted by the Communists from that time on, but had no clue the house was bugged.

Dr. Takacs and the young men were held in this cell where there were only two beds for the 15 to 20 people. Many were held there for up to one year before their trials. They had to rotate, 15 minutes on a bed then off so the next person could get his turn. There was one bucket in the corner for their toilet. The Doctor was held here for about six months before the family heard or saw anything of him. They didn't know if he was still alive or not.

House of Terror

The building in which he was held was 60 Andrassy Boulevard, then the secret police headquarters for the Communist government, today known as the House of Terror. Made into a museum in 2002, it tells the story Dr. Takacs and other prisoners who were fortunate enough to survive its horror were afraid to tell their families. If a family member was overheard discussing such an issue, that person could then be hauled in for interrogation and possible torture. Better to keep quiet about what had been done to you.

> Here the security officers killed without hesitation and forced confessions or executed without trial. Thousands were killed here. The authority took over almost the entire block and joined together the basements of all the buildings it controlled. Beneath the ground was an elaborate maze of prison, torture and execution. ... After the suppressed Uprise of 1956, thousands were imprisoned, tortured, and executed in the House of Terror.[101]

First Visit!

One day Rose was at work in the Medical building when someone secretly called to tell her that if she and her mother could get there before 11:00 AM, the two of them would be able to see her father. It was now 9:30. Rose ran frantically to where her mother was working, and together they ran to the jail.

They watched with heavy hearts as this man they loved so dearly came shuffling along, unshaven and trembling, with fingernails like claws. He was wearing shoes that were tied on with string wrapped around and around them, flopping with each step he took. They were able to talk with him through a screen, but could not touch him.

Rose managed to remain under control as long as he was in sight, but when he was carried away again, she began screaming at the top of her lungs, "I hate every Communist! I want them all dead!" Her mother couldn't control her, but managed to get her out of the area without her being arrested.

Trial

The next year, there was a sham trial where Dr. Takacs was not allowed to call any witnesses on his behalf, nor was he allowed to hire a lawyer of his choice. The family had frantically called everyone they knew to try and get legal help for him, but no one was allowed to help. The Communist government chose a lawyer for him, and the government called witnesses to testify against him.

The lawyer, though chosen by the Communists, was a good and kind Jewish man. The family saw that he did what he could in impossible circumstances and thanked him. He told the family that one day there would be a regime change, and maybe they would be able to return the favor and help him at that time.

This lawyer kindly let the family know when the Doctor's trial would take place. The family was not allowed in the courtroom to watch the closed, sham trial. They sat on benches in the hallway and could see him as he was brought by the guards in for the trial and when he was brought out of the courtroom to be returned to the jail.

At first the doctor's sentence was death. This could have been carried out swiftly, but the lawyer appealed and managed to get his sentence changed to life in prison.

Prison

After his trial and sentencing, Dr. Takacs was transferred to a prison outside of Budapest. God had plans to make his confinement there a bit easier. His prison guard related to the doctor how his wife was dying from an undiagnosed illness, her doctors baffled by her symptoms with no idea of how to help her. Dr. Takacs told him to bring her in to the prison where he could examine her. On examination, Dr. Takacs told her exactly what was wrong and what must be done. Can you imagine her gratitude and her husband's gratitude when she made a total recovery? To show their gratitude, she cooked a tremendous meal for the doctor. The guard slipped the food in to the doctor, the bulk of which was shared with other half-starved inmates.

"Because the Lord was with him, and that which he did, the Lord made it to prosper" (KJV Gen. 39:23b).[102]

Reminiscent of Joseph in the Bible: sold into slavery by his brothers, falsely accused by the wife of his new master, and thrown into prison. There in the prison, God gave him great wisdom, *"and showed him mercy, and gave him favor in the sight of the keeper of the prison"* (KJV Gen. 39:21b).[103]

This prison had a Medical Facility, and the doctors who were taking care of the inmates there would often request that Dr. Takacs be allowed to assist them with their heavy workload. This was a tremendous blessing for Dr. Takacs, so much better than sitting all day in his cell. These doctors could only give him a cigarette or a cup of coffee in return for his services, but the occasional work made the time go faster.

Back at Home

After the doctor was taken to prison, the Communist authorities moved a family of Gypsies and a family connected to the AUT, the Hungarian equivalent to the KGB, into his house. Now Rose's family (her mother, Attila, and Zsuzsy), had three rooms and one bathroom. Her mother was forced to cook in the hallway. Rose told her mother they should always hold their heads up high and not give the Communists the satisfaction of knowing they had hurt them. The Takacses also attempted to maintain their healthy sense of humor, even in the most trying circumstances.

The photo below shows brave faces, but also reveals the sadness felt by missing Dr. Takacs, who was in prison, and missing Ferenc, Paul, and Zsolt, who had all fled the country.

Rose, Mother Rozsa, Zsuzsy, Attila[104]

In 1957, after Dr. Takacs had been imprisoned, Zsuzsy was not allowed to attend school in Budapest because her father was "an outcast, the enemy of the state." Her mother contacted the authorities in the Catholic school for girls in Debrecan and pleaded with them to allow her entrance there. They did, and she studied there for seven years, graduating when she was 18.

Zsuzsy Takacs[105]

The Communists made a show of allowing one Catholic and one Reformed Presbyterian school to remain as such in the country to prove how magnanimous they were. This was the Catholic school Zsuzsy attended. The other Catholic and Protestant schools now became the public schools.

Attila

Young Attila Takacs had become very depressed with the life they were forced to live under Communist rule. His brothers were gone and his father in prison. He was 15 years old and felt he had no hope and no future. He told his mother, "I'm not going back to school. There's no use in it." Fortunately he was still allowed to attend school since he had already started High School, as Zsuzsy was not.

His mother insisted that he was going back, and that he would get the best education he could. Unenthused, he finished High School, but knew he wouldn't be allowed to enroll in the University. He found a job as a technician, doing sewing machine repairs, in the building next to the family's home. This had one bright spot, though, as he met his future wife, Anna ("Anci"), there.

Visits

Dr. Takacs was allowed to have one family member visit him for one-half hour every six months. Naturally, his wife was the one to go. Seeing him through the partition, unable to touch him, his distraught wife kept her chin up and tried to be cheerful. At least this was better than the long months with no news where she could only imagine his suffering, not knowing whether he was dead or alive.

Rose had always had such a loving bond with her father. When she was just two years old, her father was away one night, and Rose cried uncontrollably. Her mother didn't know what was wrong and tried everything she could to calm her. Finally, as her mother walked with her, they came in front of a picture of her father. As Rose looked at the picture, she immediately quieted down and dropped off to sleep. Her love and admiration for her father knew no bounds. Now knowing he had done no wrong, indeed he had done so much good, and seeing him be so mistreated, was almost more than she could bear.

One day a patient came to the Medical Building where Rose worked and told her he had seen her father receiving radiation for cancer. The family had not been told he had cancer and had no idea how advanced it might be. Rose managed to talk to the Radiologist and learned that it was Thyroid Cancer. Her father had been beaten around the neck as he was being tortured, the Communists trying to persuade him to give evidence against other people.

One day the Radiologist at the National Cancer Institute secretly notified Rose to get her mother and come to the Radiology Department and he would arrange for them to see her father. Being very careful not to attract undue attention to themselves, they entered separately, and the Radiologist took Rozsa into the room where radiation was usually administered. Rose's father was on a bed, ready to receive his treatment. The doctor had Rozsa lie on a bed next to his, pretending she was also a patient receiving treatment. Then he closed the door on the room and told everyone to stay outside because radiation was being given. He had not turned on the machine, of course, and just allowed Rose's parents a few minutes to talk.

Meanwhile, Rose waited in the Radiologist's office. See page 123 in Attila's story to see what transpired next.

Provision

One day Rose was at work when she received a call to come to the National Cancer Institute for a job. When she arrived, the Personnel Officer said, "We can't hire her! She's not a Communist!" The doctor who had asked her to come was adamant: "If she can do the job, I don't care if she's a monkey. She CAN do the job. Hire her now!" So, they did. She now had to work just six hours a day and was paid a higher salary than the men around her—God's provision for her and her family.

Rozsa had tried to find employment, but she had two strikes against her: she was not a Communist, and she was part of a privileged class. The government thought it would be better if she would just die. In fear of the government, no one would hire her. Finally, one of Dr.

Takacs's former patients who ran a peach orchard secretly hired her to pick peaches, though this was seasonal and temporary. Later she got a job serving ice cream during the summer, and then serving at a coffee shop, always for minimum wage, and it always had to be done without the government knowing.

Rose's income was the real support for the family. Such was their economic condition that Rose once worked an entire year to earn enough to purchase a warm winter coat. Not fur, not leather, just a warm cloth coat, though she was now the Assistant to the Director at the Cancer Institute and had her own office where she studied tissue samples under the microscope, particularly bone marrow samples, and provided other valuable assistance to the Director.

Nurse Imposter

When her father was to have an operation, the surgeon secretly told Rose she could come in to see her father, disguised in a nurse's uniform he had hidden for her to wear. Since others were there, the only thing Rose was able to do for her father was give him a cup of tea and pat his head. He saw her and knew she was there for him, though neither of them could say a word for fear of her identity being discovered. Unfortunately, someone who was there recognized her and reported her being a nurse imposter. Because of this, instead of being able to remain in the hospital for three or four days after his surgery and have nursing care to recover, her father was sent immediately back to the prison.

Freedom!

In the early 1960s Janos Kadar (Prime Minister and General Secretary of the Hungarian Communist Party) announced a new policy: He declared a general amnesty, gradually curbed some of the excesses of the secret police ... private ownership was not banned anymore ... products like Coca Cola and blue jeans were available in the shops. ... Travelling abroad became easier, though dissidents and opponents of the system still remained closely watched by the secret police, particularly during the anniversaries of the 1956 uprising.[106]

In 1963, an Amnesty was brokered by the United States, and political prisoners were released, Dr. Takacs among them.

Though Dr. Takacs's health was severely damaged, he would live another fourteen years. No one had dared hope that he would come out of prison alive, first because he had a life sentence, and second because he had suffered two heart attacks and had Leukemia and Thyroid Cancer. When he was released, his doctor said he might live another three years. The harsh prison life had aggravated all of these medical conditions, so his family considered that they had been granted a precious miracle when he survived and lived on.

After Dr. Takacs had returned to his home, a Catholic priest, Fr. Adam, who had testified against him, came to the home to see him. This was a priest who lived across the street and had been in the Takacses's home many times, talking with the doctor. Dr. Takacs and Rozsa were upstairs and looked down to see the priest enter downstairs. The priest fell to his knees and in tears pleaded with the doctor, "Please forgive me. I'm so sorry!"

Though the priest's testimony against him had hurt him badly, Dr. Takacs's reply was typical of his attitude toward all people. "Everyone can make a mistake. It's okay. Come on in, and let's have a cup of coffee."

He always chided any family member if they expressed hatred for anyone. He always said that God made people good, so there is good somewhere inside of everyone. We just need to look for the good. All of his actions for all of his life reflected this attitude. A Man Among Men, the Gold Standard.

Chapter Twelve:
Rose Takacs Little:
Coming to America

Rose continued working at the Cancer Institute, and in 1968, she spent her year's salary paying a lawyer to get passports for her parents and permission for them to leave Communist Hungary and travel to America. Not knowing whether this could actually be done or not, Rose kept her plan a secret from her parents. It took many months to get the documents, and Rose joyously wanted to celebrate when they finally came. When she told her parents they had a cause to celebrate with champagne, they couldn't imagine what she meant. Then she told them. It was too good for them to believe. They had one son in Canada and two in America they had not seen for years. There were grandchildren they had never seen. They had longed to make the trip to America, but couldn't see how it would ever be possible. The doctor was afraid it was too good to be true, that he would wake up and find it a dream, but in 1969, they came and remained for a year.

What a wonderful year! The doctor loved everything about America. Meanwhile back in Hungary, the family's youngest daughter, Zsuzsy, married to Huba Nemeshanyi, had a baby girl Rozsa was longing to see. The doctor understood and agreed to return home, realizing they might never be allowed to leave again.

In 1972, Rose came to America. It was hard for anyone to get a passport, and the name Takacs would make it harder. Rose was married at this time, so the name used was not Takacs. Her boss at the Cancer Institute helped make it possible for her to come and made promises to the authorities that she would return. He had vouched for her, so he asked her to please not get him in trouble by staying, so she returned after one month.

Christmas 1974

Rose had prayed: "Please God, let us have the whole family together for one more Christmas." In 1974, Father, Mother, Rose, Zsuzsy, and Attila all came from Hungary to Silver Spring, MD to Paul and Terezia's, their house always being the focal point of family gatherings in the US. Frank and Helen came from Canada, and Zsolt and Ruth came from Ohio. The entire family would have been together for Christmas, as Rose had prayed, except Hungary's Communist government required Zsuzsy and Attila's spouses and children to remain behind. This would guarantee that these two would return, which they did after about a month.

Front Row: Zsolt, Mother Rozsa, Dr. Takacs
Back Row: Attila, Zsuzsy, Paul, Frank, Rose

Defection

Rose had married in Hungary, but had divorced after seven years. When her parents and her brother and sister returned to Hungary in 1974, she remained behind, defected, intending to stay permanently in the US. She lived with Paul and Terezia in Silver Spring, MD at first.

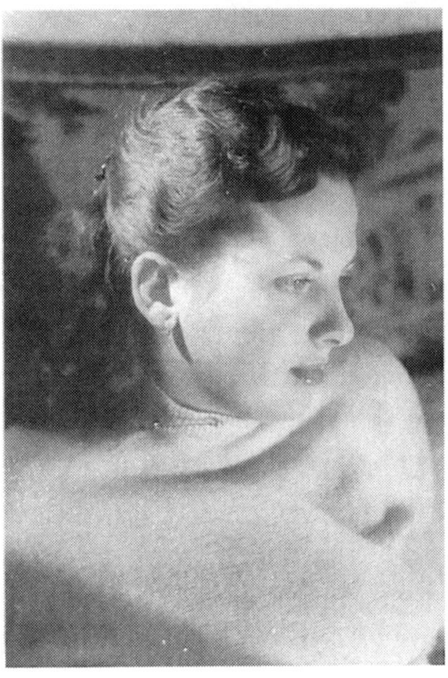

Rose

Her parents back in Hungary were thoroughly questioned by the authorities because she had not returned. People who left the country without permission of the Communist government always knew any family left in Hungary could possibly be punished because of their defection. Rose's parents told the authorities that she was a grown woman, and they had no control over her whereabouts, though they had given Rose their blessing to remain in America. Dr. Takacs had even instructed Rose's brothers to look after her.

Rose said it took many years of living in the US before she stopped looking over her shoulder to see who might be listening when she answered questions for anyone. Her brothers would remind her, "Rose, you're in America!"

She wanted to find a job, though she spoke no English. A friend of Paul and Terzia's learned a job was available at the Holy Cross Hospital, so she went with Rose to apply. The friend assured the hospital of Rose's credentials and ability, so she got the job. Again she was working as a Medical Assistant, doing the work she had done in this position in

Hungary. She worked there part time for about a year before moving to the office of a Hungarian doctor.

Enter Paul Little

One day she was in the hallway of the office of the Hungarian doctor when she saw a man a few feet away, looking at her. Distracted, he bumped his head on an overhead pipe, to which Rose remarked in his hearing, "Idiot!" Back in the office a few minutes later, the doctor came proudly bringing this man in to introduce him to Rose, calling him his good friend. Embarrassed? This awkward beginning soon led to love, Rose and the man she had called "idiot" were married about two years later, and with this marriage, Rose became an American citizen.

Paul Yates Little, far from being an idiot, was both a medical doctor and a lawyer. He had been a professor who taught Law at the American University in Washington, DC. He had also worked briefly for a congressman on Capitol Hill, but now he was retired.

Dr. Paul and Rose Little[107]

Rose and Paul Little made the trip to Hungary in 1979 to visit members of Rose's family still living there. Paul had met her mother when she visited in the US. Rose was still a Hungarian citizen, and the authorities told her she could visit, but if she broke any laws, she would not have the courtesy shown to foreigners but would be punished as any other Hungarian. If she wanted to rescind her Hungarian citizenship, she could do so for the price of $19,000. She still has dual citizenship today.

Paul went with Rose when she applied for a job in Washington, DC, working for a medical practice with four doctors. Paul knew Rose was a bit timid and thought she might not recommend herself highly enough, so he was determined to do that for her. He was very outgoing and never met a stranger, so he knew his presence would help make everyone more comfortable.

She got the job and was highly valued by the four doctors. Sadly, after five years of marriage, Paul Little died of cancer in 1984. Rose continued to work for these doctors for another year and a half, then moved to Jacksonville, FL where Zsolt and his family were living.

Jacksonville, FL

When she left the practice in Washington after five years, the doctors wrote glowing Letters of Recommendation for her, hoping she would be employed by the Mayo Clinic in Jacksonville. Mayo wanted her to go back to college for two additional years, however, so she declined.

She had had her fill of sickness and disease, so she decided to try and get a job in retail sales rather than return to the medical field. She began applying at stores in Regency Square Mall and eventually came to JC Penney's. When the employee interviewing her asked if she had experience in selling cosmetics, her answer was, "No, but I like them, so I can sell them." She was hired to sell cosmetics on commission. She outsold the younger girls who had no foreign accents and who were aggressive about approaching customers. Rose was quieter and never pressured the customers, so they sought her out. She did this successfully for 15 years, finally retiring in 2000 at the age of 65.

Church

After moving to Jacksonville, Rose wanted to find a church she would be comfortable in. While driving down St. John's Bluff Road, she spotted a church building that was a bit old, and fairly small. It reminded her of her church in Hungary, so she decided to give it a try.

When she entered the vestibule on Sunday, she heard, "Well, I guess God is teaching me a lesson. He told me to invite you to church when I bought cosmetics from you yesterday." It was one of her customers.

She soon met the pastor, Dr. Larry (Parson) Carson, and his wife, Elaine. Elaine worked as Director of World Relief in Jacksonville, helping the many refugees coming from trouble spots all over the world to get settled here. Sometimes she needed to find someone to take in a refugee family until a house or apartment could be found and furnished for them. She asked Rose if she would be willing to temporarily take in a young Russian couple, the wife being well advanced in pregnancy. Rose was taken aback at being asked to do such a thing: "I hate Russians! I can't take them into my house!" To which Elaine replied, "Now Rose, you know God doesn't want us to harbor hatred in our hearts."

Rose was soon persuaded and welcomed the young couple in. Predictably, she grew to love them, giving them many of the items they would need for their apartment and for the soon-to-be-born baby. They only stayed a month and were moved to their permanent housing, but such was the bond between them and Rose that when their baby daughter was born, she was named "Rose."

These were people fleeing Communist oppression in Russia, just as she had fled Communist oppression in Hungary. Her heart went out to them and to all other refugees fleeing similar conditions.

Later, some friends took Rose to visit their church, where she had a very personal experience with Jesus, thereafter knowing for all time that she was born-again and having a very personal daily walk with Him.

Chapter Thirteen:
Ferenc (Frank)

Paul and Zsolt left Austria for America as soon as possible, but Ferenc chose to stay in Vienna for a while to work and earn enough money to pay someone to secret his girlfriend, Helen, out of Hungary to freedom.

In the meantime, Helen was spending a lot of her time at the Takacses's house because it was in a safer location than her home in the downtown area, and there were continual flare-ups of fighting. One day when she was there, the phone rang, and it was for her. She answered and turned pale, hurriedly explaining to the family that she had to go because Ferenc was sending someone to lead her to Austria. The family wondered if this could be a trick, and she would be arrested instead. Some unscrupulous person could have taken Ferenc's money and planned to kill her instead of going to the trouble to get her to Austria. Still, they had to let her go.

She made it safely out of Hungary and joined Ferenc in Vienna. They chose to go to Canada and were married there, Ferenc thereafter being called "Frank."

Ferenc (Frank) and Helen Takacs[108]

Canada

They lived first in Toronto and then Ottowa. When Helen applied for a job, the young man who received her application was a fellow Hungarian from Budapest. He recognized the name Takacs and recommended her for employment. As she talked with him, she learned that he was a son of the railroad official who had been fired because he refused to stop attending church. He maintained a relationship with Helen and Frank for the rest of their lives, and he now communicates with Rose.

Frank's dream had been to become a doctor like his father. In Canada, he graduated from McGill University and became a Microbiologist instead. Working for the Nestle and 7UP companies, he had a very successful career, being granted four patents for developments he perfected. He was accepted as a member of Mensa, an organization composed of those in the highest two percent of intelligence in the world. This came as no surprise to the family, as they had long recognized his brilliance.

Jacksonville

In 2011, Rose was notified that Frank's wife, Helen, had broken a hip and was hospitalized in Canada. Frank was in the beginning stages of Alzheimer's and would have to go into a Nursing Home. Rose and Zsolt flew to Canada, spent a week visiting with Helen, then brought Frank back with them to Jacksonville, Florida. When Helen was better and able to travel, she joined him, but was not satisfied being away from their home and their friends. After about a month, Zsolt and Huba, who was visiting from Hungary, took them back to Canada to select an Assisted Living facility for them. In the car, on the way to one facility, Huba noticed Helen had slumped over and was unresponsive. Zsolt pulled into a hospital, where Helen was pronounced dead. Now Frank was brought back to Florida to live with Rose.

Zsolt visited with Frank almost every day when he could. Zsuzsy and Huba came from Hungary for extended stays twice and helped with his care, but taking care of Frank found Rose being very confined, since she couldn't leave him alone. By this time, she was attending

Christ the Redeemer Church in Ponte Vedra. There she met Rev. Linda and Roy Parker, who proved to be a Godsend to her and to Frank. They would come and stay with Frank while Rose left to grocery shop or run other necessary errands. They didn't just sit with him, they interacted with him in very positive ways. One day Rose returned to find Linda dancing Frank around the kitchen, which caused Frank to say to Linda, "You're alright. You must be Hungarian!"

When Frank could no longer do it for himself, Roy would shave him. When he could no longer move himself, Roy would lift him.

Pastor David Sheffield from Christ the Redeemer Church was a great source of support and blessing to Rose and Frank. He visited and spent time talking with Frank and prayed for him. He had Rev. Bowen Slade bring Communion to Frank and Rose each week, though Frank had trouble adjusting to this informal way of taking Communion, it being such a sacred ordinance of the church. Pastor David visited him when he was in the hospital and when he was in Rehab. At the end, he prayed for Frank and released him into the hands of Jesus. What a comfort this was to Rose. Pastor David has been a strong shoulder for Rose to lean on.

During the four years Frank lived with Rose, since Rose couldn't leave him to attend church, her friend at church, Auleen Harris, came to visit her every week, just to encourage her and brighten her day.

In 2015, Frank fell and had surgery for a broken hip, remaining in the hospital for three weeks. He was doing well, so he was sent to a Rehab facility. There he fell out of bed three times and died two days after Hospice took over.

Frank had a Hungarian friend in Canada who had called him every night in Jacksonville to discuss world news. When Frank died, this friend, Kalman Gondocz, a 96-year-old retired Reformed Presbyterian pastor, told Rose he would now have no one to talk to. Rose told him she couldn't talk every night, but he could call now and then, and she would be glad to talk with him. When he calls every Thursday night, they speak Hungarian and discuss world news. Gondocz had left Hungary as a young man to study at a Seminary in Holland, but still has a great love for his native land.

Chapter Fourteen:
Attila

The Picture

Dr. Takacs knew of Attila's discouragement when he saw his father taken to prison and of his conviction that finishing High School was of no value as long as they were living under the oppressive Communist regime. Dr. Takacs desperately wanted Attila to get as much education as he could, beginning with finishing High School. With communications between the family and the father in prison being so limited, he couldn't know for months at the time whether his son had dropped out of school or not.

Rozsa and Rose were insisting to Attila that he would continue in school if they had to carry him there themselves. When he did graduate, he made a cardboard sign saying, "I graduated," and Rose took his picture, hoping to be able to use it to get the news to his father.

When the Radiologist arranged for Rose and her mother to be able to see her father (see page 110), Rose took this picture, along with others, hoping to find a way to show them to her father. She didn't know how this could be done, since the guard who was bringing her father for a radiation treatment knew the family wasn't supposed to visit with him.

Rose sat in the office of the Radiologist while her mother was in the Radiation room, pretending to receive a treatment. Rose showed the Radiologist the pictures and explained how much she had hoped to show them to her father. When the guard came by, taking Dr. Takacs back to his cell, the Radiologist stood up and said to the guard, "Let me show you some beautiful pictures. Don't you think these are wonderful?" He held them so that Dr. Takacs could see them, too. This allowed Dr. Takacs to see the picture of Attila with the message that he had indeed graduated.

Attila: "I graduated"[109]

Attila was the family comedian. He would say hilarious things and keep a solemn look on his face as others rolled on the floor in laughter. He always made any family gathering more fun.

Anci and Attila[110]

Adult Life

Attila worked for the government as a sewing machine repairman until he was near retirement age. Two years before he was eligible for retirement with government benefits for the remainder of his life, the government terminated his employment and therefore ended their obligation to pay him retirement income. This left him with nothing with which to live. When he learned this, Zsolt flew to Budapest and personally established a fund for Attila and Anci, which provided for them both, and since Attila's death continues to provide for Anci.

Attila and Anci have two children, Attila and Aniko. Attila died from an aneurism in 2013 at the age of 70. He had consulted his doctor about abdominal pain, but the doctor did no tests and told him to watch what he ate, never suspecting an aneurism. Attila's entire family was together for a wonderful laughter-filled visit in 2013. Attila went to take a shower and go to bed, saying goodnight to all. He was found dead the next morning.

Chapter Fifteen: Zsuzsanna

By the early 1980s some lasting economic reforms and limited political liberalization were achieved. ... Hungary remained committed to a pro-Soviet foreign policy and openly criticized US President Ronald Reagan's deployment of intermediate-range nuclear missiles in Europe. In 1986, Reagan's proposed visit to Hungary was refused by Janos Kadar, as he [Reagan] criticized firmly the policy of the Soviet block, and was the greatest opponent of the communist system, declaring his task as "bringing the Cold War to a conclusion, and regaining Hungary's sovereignty in the process."[111]

Zsuzanna, "Zsuzsy," the youngest of the Takacs children, lived on in Hungary, working as a librarian in Hungary's National Library, similar to the Library of Congress in the US.

Zsuzsy and Huba[112]

In 1982 her husband, Huba Nemeshanyi, a Hydro Engineer, was sent to the Middle East for a few years. Zsuzsy and their children lived there with him in Yemen and Kuwait for three years until he was returned to Hungary. Back in Hungary, Zsuzsy now worked as a school librarian. When Huba was sent back to the Middle East, Zsuzsy realized her mother needed her, as she had been diagnosed with Parkinson's Disease, and her health had deteriorated. Zsuzsy stayed in Hungary and took care of her until she died in 1995.

Huba has published a wonderful encyclopedia-like book in Hungarian about his family, the Nemeshanyis, and the Takacs family. Many of the pictures in this book are included in the huge number he collected for his publication.

Huba has quite a story, too. His father, an officer in the Hungarian army, was captured by the Russians and sent to prison months before Huba was born. Since his father died there, Huba never knew him. As an adult, Huba met a 102-year-old man who had been in prison with his father and who told him many things about his father he would otherwise never have known. This elderly man had been imprisoned by the Russians for 30 years, and was finally released, only to be imprisoned again for a year and a half when he reached the Hungarian border. Miraculously, he harbors no bitterness. He and Huba have developed a very close relationship, with him as sort of a surrogate father, filling the place of the father Huba never knew.

Zsuzsy and Huba have a vacation home on the lake that afforded the Takacs children so much enjoyment during childhood summers. The two of them live there from August to October each year. Rose enjoys going back to Hungary during this time for six to eight weeks for family reunions there at the lake.

Zsuzsy and Huba have two children, Zsuzsy and Balazs.

Mother Rozsa, Zsuzsy, Daughter Zsuzsy, Balazs 1984[113]

Epilogue

Soviet Union Collapsing

By late 1988 activists within the Communist Party and bureaucracy and Budapest-based intellectuals were increasing pressure for change. Young liberals formed the Federation of Young Democrats ... and the national opposition established the Hungarian Democratic Forum. In 1988 Janos Kadar resigned. One year later, in 1989, the Parliament adopted a "democracy package" which included trade union pluralism; freedom of association, assembly, and the press; furthermore a new electoral law. In August 1989 ... the Iron Curtain was cut over Hungary. The Iron Curtain wasn't just a phrase ... it was literally a guarded, roughly 7000 km long wirefence barrier, spotted with watchtowers, which millions of people couldn't cross because they were imprisoned in their home countries. ... Hungarians could now leave for Austria.

The Soviet Union reduced its involvement by signing an agreement in April 1989 to withdraw Soviet forces by June 1991.

In June 1989 ... the country reburied Imre Nagy, his associates, and symbolically all other victims of the 1956 Revolution.

In October 1989, the Communist Party convened its last congress and re-established itself as the Hungarian Socialist Party. ... The Parliament adopted legislation providing for multiparty parliamentary elections ... transformed Hungary from a People's Republic into the Republic of Hungary, guaranteed human and civil rights, and created an institutional structure that ensures separation of powers among the judicial, executive, and legislative branches of government. On 23rd October 1989 (on the 33rd anniversary of the Revolution of 1956), the present Republic of Hungary was proclaimed on Kossuth Square in Budapest. ... Hungary strengthened its ties with Western Europe; in May 2004, Hungary became a member of the European Union.[114]

Though he never visited there, on June 29, 2011, a statue of former U.S. President Ronald Reagan was unveiled in the center of Liberty Square in Budapest. It is there because the people of Hungary wanted to show their appreciation for his effectiveness in ending the Cold War, which put an end to the USSR's influence in Hungary. [115]

The Family

Zoltan and Matilde Eordogh's son, Bertalan, Rozsa's brother, died of starvation as a Prisoner of War in France during World War II. A fellow prisoner who had been freed brought the news to his parents, along with their son's journal and a crust of bread. Bertalan had carried this crust of bread from home, from a loaf his mother had baked, and had kept it throughout his time in battle and prison. In his journal he had recorded such heartbreaking notes as "We had only hot water for our dinner," and "We can see the women walking by on the street carrying loaves of bread, taunting us." He had been in High School when he was drafted into a youth corps and sent off to fight, being soon captured. War is truly Hell for both sides.

Matilde found herself unable to eat for days. The family feared she, too, would die of starvation. When they tried to coax her to eat, she replied, "How can I eat and enjoy food when my child died because he was denied food?" Dr. Takacs was finally able to persuade her to eat and live. She lived until 1981.

Bertalan's Remains in Box 55, in France[116]

Bertalan's sister, Katalin, is trying to have his remains returned to the family.

Dr. Pal Takacs died in 1977 in the Cancer Institute in Budapest from Coronary Disease. He also had endured Heart Attacks, Leukemia, and Thyroid Cancer. The next year, the government tore down the Takacses's house, saying it was no longer safe. Mother Rozsa had to find a place to live. The Communist government wanted her out of District 22 where the family was so well known and loved, but she managed to find an apartment there, anyway. It was in an apartment house, on the third floor, across from the elevator. There was an alcove with a door on the right and one on the left. On the left, the door led to a one-bedroom apartment for Rozsa, and on the right, a two-bedroom apartment for Huba, Zsuzsy, and their children.

Mother Rozsa died in 1995 from Parkinson's Disease. Rose had prayed that, after all her parents had been through, they would not have to bury any of their children. God answered that prayer.

Paul died in 2000. He had Prostate Cancer which had spread over his body, causing excruciating pain. On August 20, 2000, unable to endure the pain any longer, he took his own life.

Attila died from an aneurism in 2013.

Frank died from Alzheimer's Disease in 2015.

Dr. Pal Takacs Honored

The national leadership of the Reformed Presbyterian Church had been pushing the government of Hungary to give some recognition to the contributions of Dr. Pal Takacs, so in 2015, the government awarded him Hungary's Medal of Freedom.

In Budapest, the "Dr. Takacs Pal Park" was established on the land that had once held his home before it was torn down by the authorities in 1978.[117]

Huba, Zsuzsy and the Reformed Church Superintendent at the Park[118]

Park Dedication[119]

In 2016, the government also placed a plaque on the Medical Building, just outside of the window that was in Dr. Takacs's office. The plaque reads:

> Dr. Pal Takacs, 1900-1977, treated and healed people here. The whole of Budafok esteemed and loved him as their extremely outstanding doctor. After the Glorious Uprising in 1956, he was sentenced to a lifetime in prison. After six years, he was freed by the amnesty.

In his book, *The Bridge at Andau*, James Michener quoted an American diplomat who helped some of the Freedom Fighters and other Hungarian citizens escape the horrors of Communist cruelty into freedom in Austria during the revolt of 1956: "When this pressure lets up, I just want one thing: A transfusion of Hungarian blood. I want to feel like a man again."[120]

He was that impressed by the raw courage of the brave Hungarians who had stood up against the savage reign of terror inflicted upon their country by the Russian Communists.

Rose frequently goes back to Hungary for long visits and reunions. During these trips, she always visited Jenny Strausser in Vienna until

Jenny died in 2010. Jenny was deeply loved by the entire family and had their undying gratitude.

Rose was asked if she wanted to see the Museum of Horror, since that was the place her father was held until after his trial. The very thought of it brings back too much terror for her to even consider it.

The Alba Regia Chapel

The ashes of Paul, Frank, and Helen are secured on the grounds of The Alba Regia Chapel at Mount Tabor in Berkeley Springs, West Virginia. Built and maintained by the Hungarian Freedom Fighters Federation, this is the final resting place of many Hungarians from all over the world. "The grounds are dotted with symbolic graves commemorating the heroes of the 1956 Revolution and soldiers who have defended Hungary through the centuries."[121]

The Alba Regia Chapel[122]

An intricate wrought-iron gate, designed by Paul Takacs, leads to the underground mausoleum.

Wrought Iron Gate Designed by Paul Takacs[123]

Paul's Ashes[124]

"There are also memorials to the Hungarians who fought in the American Revolution and the Civil War, simple but powerful reminders of the intertwined histories of the United States and Hungary."[125] The chapel is a symbol of Hungarian tenacity and will to survive and a tribute to the "many who founded and rebuilt, defended and reconquered, converted and reconverted the nation," and "provides a glimpse of the major triumphs and tragedies the country has experienced throughout her rich and tumultuous past."[126]

Our Debt to Hungary

Europe is deeply indebted to Hungary, which made many sacrifices to protect the safety of the west. For centuries this small group of herdsmen, only recently from Asia themselves, fought off subsequent waves of invading Mongols, who otherwise would have ransacked Paris and Rome. Later it was the Hungarians who bore the brunt of Europe's fight against the Muslims of Turkey, refusing to relinquish either the Christian religion, which they had adopted around the year 1000, or their European way of life.[127]

Life Goes On

Today, Rose, Zsolt, and Zsuzsy remain, rejoicing to see a free and independent Hungary, with its population of almost 10 million, "Rising like the Phoenix from the ashes," as Zsolt says.

America the Beautiful

For Rose and Zsolt, America is home. Their patriotic love for and devotion to their adopted country knows no bounds. Only those who have known the bondage they have known can so deeply appreciate the freedom America affords to the "masses yearning to breathe free."[128]

Footnotes

1   The Florida Times-Union Jacksonville Journal newspaper, October 28, 1979.
2   Zsolt B. Takacs, "Hungary's Movement Toward a Market-Based Economy After the Collapse of Communism" (Thesis: LaSalle University).
3   Budapest.Com: 9/7/17.
4   Funk & Wagnalls New Encyclopedia, Vol. 13 (US: Funk & Wagnalls, Inc., 1983), 293.
5   Ibid.
6   CBN News program, "Jerusalem Dateline," broadcast on GOD TV, August 28, 2017.)
7   Funk & Wagnalls, 294-296.
8   Ibid., 296.
9   Nemeshanyi Huba, Nemeshanyi-Takacs Legendarium (Budapest, Hungary, 2014), 116.
10 Ibid., 115.
11 Ibid., 119.
12 Ibid., 109.
13 Ibid.
14 Ibid., 108.
15 Ibid., 110.
16 Ibid., 136.
17 Ibid., 137.
18 Ibid.
19 Ibid.
20 Ibid., 136.
21 Ibid., 134.
22 Funk and Wagnalls 297.
23 Nemeshanyi, 122.
24 Funk and Wagnalls 297.
25 Collage Dalma, (Oslo, Norway: 2014), n.p.
26 Ibid.

[27] Nemeshanyi, 126.

[28] Ibid 129.

[29] Ibid 131.

[30] Ibid 132.

[31] Funk and Wagnall's, 297-298.

[32] Nemeshanyi, 144.

[33] Ibid.

[34] Ibid., 145.

[35] Ibid.

[36] Funk and Wagnalls, 298.

[37] C. Peter Chen, World War II Database, Internet.

[38] Ibid.

[39] Nemeshanyi, 146.

[40] Holy Bible: New King James Version (Nashville Camden New York: Thomas Nelson Publishers, 1982).

[41] Ibid.

[42] Ibid.

[43] World Book Encyclopedia, Vol. H (Chicago London Rome Sydney Toronto: Field Enterprises Educational Corporation, 1970), 392.

[44] Funk & Wagnalls, 298.

[45] Ibid.

[46] Ibid.

[47] World Book, 396-397.

[48] "Flag of Hungary." Wikipedia.

[49] Ibid.

[50] Collage Dalma.

[51] "Flag of Hungary." Wikipedia.

[52] Ibid.

[53] Ibid.

[54] Ibid.

[55] Ibid.

[56] Collage Dalma.

[57] "Coat of Arms of Hungary." Wikipedia.

[58] Ibid.

[59] James A. Michener, The Bridge At Andau (New York: Fawcett

Crest, 1957), 1.

60 Ibid., 4.

61 Ibid., 201.

62 Ibid., 31.

63 Ibid., 54-55.

64 Ibid., 56.

65 Ibid., 77.

66 Ibid., 56.

67 Ibid., 78.

68 Ibid., 101.

69 Ibid., 95.

70 Ibid., 102-103.

71 Ibid., 103.

72 Ibid., 101.

73 Ibid., 97.

74 Ibid., 101-102.

75 Ibid., 168.

76 Ibid., 164.

77 Ibid.

78 Ibid., 170.

79 Collage Dalma.

80 Holy Bible: New King James Version.

81 Nemeshanyi, 169.

82 Takacs, Terezia: Takacs, A Sketch Book in Memory of Paul Takacs (Silver Spring, Maryland, 2001), 13.

83 Ibid., 12.

84 Nemeshanyi, 165.

85 Takacs, Terezia, 3.

86 Ibid., 7.

87 Ibid., 23.

88 Ibid.

89 Ibid., 5.

90 Elemer Bako, "Fidelissimus ad Mortem" (Unveiling and Dedication Ceremony of the Statue of Colonel Commandant Michael Kovats de Fabricy) October 11, 2003.

91 Takacs, Terezia, 57.

92 Ibid., 6.

93 Ibid.

94 Ibid.

95 Ibid., 13.

96 Ibid., 20.

97 Holy Bible: New King James Version.

98 Nemeshanyi, 174.

99 Zsolt B. Takacs.

100 Funk and Wagnall's Dictionary, p. 146.

101 "History of Hungary Museums," Ask.com.

102 Holy Bible: New King James Version.

103 Ibid.

104 Nemeshanyi, 163.

105 Ibid., 165.

106 "Hungary after 1956 and Today": Internet, 9/7/2017.

107 Nemeshanyi, 171.

108 Ibid., 167.

109 Ibid., 162.

110 Ibid., 175.

111 "The Way to the European Union-Hungary After 1956 and Today": Google.

112 Nemeshanyi, 180.

113 Ibid., 229.

114 "The Way to the European Union-Hungary After 1956 and Today."

115 Google.com.

116 Nemeshanyi, 130.

117 REFORMATUSOK LAPIA 2016 oktober 30 (Hungarian Newspaper).

118 Ibid.

119 Ibid.

120 Michener, 179.

121 Alba Regia Chapel, Berkeley Springs, West Virginia program.

122 Ibid.

123 Ibid.

124 Ibid.

[125] Ibid.

[126] Ibid.

[127] Michener, 184.

[128] Statue of Liberty.

Works Cited

Christian Broadcast Network News program, "Jerusalem Dateline."

Collage Dalma. Oslo, Norway, 2014.

Funk & Wagnalls New Encyclopedia, Vol. 13 (US: Funk & Wagnalls, Inc., 1983.

Gabor, Horchler. "Spirit of Hungary in West Virginia." Berkeley Springs, West Virginia, 1993.

Holy Bible: New King James Version (Nashville Camden New York: Thomas Nelson Publishers, 1982).

Michener, James A. Bridge at Andau. New York: Fawcett Crest, 1957.

Nemeshanyi, Huba. Nemeshanyi-Takacs Legends. Budapest, Hungary, 2014.

Takacs, Terezia. Takacs, A Sketch Book in Memory of Paul Takacs. Silver Spring, Maryland, 2001.

Takacs, Zsolt. "Hungary's Movement Toward a Market-Based Economy After the Collapse of Communism" (Thesis: LaSalle University).

Florida Times-Union Jacksonville Journal newspaper Sunday, October 28, 1979.

"The Way to the European Union-Hungary After 1956 and Today": Google.

World Book Encyclopedia, Vol. H. (Chicago London Rome Sydney Toronto: Field Enterprises Educational Corporation, 1970).

Other Books By Helen Jordan Davis

The Joshua Principles: How To Possess Your Promised Land

The Nehemiah Principles: Rebuild Your Wall Of Protection

The Covenant Principles: What It Means To Be In Covenant With God

The Genesis Principles: Old Testament Treasures Vol. One

The Christmas Principles: Why Christians MUST Celebrate Christmas

O-The Story of Oliver and Nadgy
(With Nadgy Drury)

Mickey-Life and Times So Far

Watchman! Have You Been Sleeping?

Everyone Has A Story-Paul Thomas Jordan
(With Paul Thomas Jordan)

He Makes All Things Beautiful In His Time
(With Yvonne Carter)

144

CPSIA information can be obtained
at www.ICGtesting.com
Printed in the USA
FFOW01n2017080618
47054058-49424FF